KOREATOWN

# KOREATOWN

코리아타운

## A COOKBOOK

### DEUKI HONG & MATT RODBARD

Photographs by Sam Horine

Clarkson Potter/Publishers
New York

Copyright © 2016 by Matt Rodbard and Deuki Hong

Photographs copyright © 2016 by Sam Horine

Published in the United States by Clarkson Potter/Publishers, an imprint of the Crown Publishing Group, a division of Penguin Random House LLC, New York.
www.crownpublishing.com
www.clarksonpotter.com

CLARKSON POTTER is a trademark and POTTER with colophon is a registered trademark of Penguin Random House LLC.

Photographs on title page and pages 38, 67, 79, 96, 111, 113, 123, 146, 152, 160, 168, 174, 179, 191, 203, 219, 225, and 237 by Gabi Porter
Photographs on pages 98, 107, and 227 by Matt Rodbard

ISBN 978-0-804-18613-1
eISBN 978-0-804-18614-8
Printed in China

Book design by La Tricia Watford
Cover design by La Tricia Watford
Cover photography by Sam Horine
Back cover photograph by Gabi Porter
Illustrations by Michael Hoeweler

10  9 8 7 6 5 4 3 2 1
First Edition

Library of Congress Cataloging-in-Publication Data
Hong, Deuki.
   Koreatown : a cookbook / Deuki Hong and Matt Rodbard ; photographs by Sam Horine. — First edition.
      pages cm
   1. Cooking, Korean.  I. Rodbard, Matt.  II. Horine, Sam.  III. Title.
   TX724.5.K65H66 2015
   641.59519—dc23
                    2015009587

# CONTENTS

# INTRODUCTION

You're holding a Korean cookbook in your hands, and there's a bright, unapologetically funky, sometimes spicy, oftentimes bubbling, impossibly interesting future awaiting you. You may know this already. Maybe you're Korean. Maybe you're married to a Korean, have a Korean best friend, adopted a Korean child, lived in Korea for a summer or just fell into a K-food hole, where you can expect a life lived entirely on bowls of Shin Ramyun and dakdoritang. Maybe you've already been hypnotized by the unexpected pleasure of samgyupsal dipped in sesame oil, or know the joy of the perfect plate of sizzling nakji bokkeum. Or maybe you're simply curious about what all these dishes are, and why millions of people are obsessed with them.

There are nearly two million people of Korean heritage living in the United States today, spread out in Koreatowns all across the country—from sprawling Los Angeles and vertically rising New York City to smaller dots on the map. In each of these communities, big and small, society revolves around clusters of restaurants that serve the traditional foods of the motherland.

For an outsider, a visit to one of these hidden little gems can be exhilarating, with the smell of cooked rice and sesame oil smacking you in the face upon entering, and the promise of a completely new restaurant experience. Mysterious bubbling pots and meats braised in soy sauce and orchard fruits. The endless parade of complimentary small plates called banchan. Korean food is never, ever, a boring time.

OK, try this: Type "Korean restaurant" into Google Maps. Chances are there's one near you. Hit "driving directions." You're that close! Or, really, you're even closer: Just keep reading.

"Our interest in Asian cuisine has exploded," says chef and well-traveled TV food personality Andrew Zimmern, allowing the *explode* to exit his mouth like a light bottle rocket. "Americans cannot get enough of it. I believe that to be true with every fiber of my being. This is why it's so frustrating for me to see that one of my all-time favorite Asian cuisines—Korean—has yet to be swept up in that bandwagon. And I am still trying to figure out why this is the case."

Well, Andrew Zimmern, we're on the case: The case to educate home cooks about the methods behind the magic of fire and fermentation, and to do our best to help popularize Korean food in America beyond kimchi tacos, fried chicken and barbecue. Those are three things we love, but there is much more to this story. And for those folks who have never had a slurp of icy naengmyeon, or spoon of doenjang jjigae, maybe we can play a role in getting you there.

From the start, when Deuki and Matt (more on us later) first met over bowls of seolleongtang on 32nd Street in Manhattan, we agreed that our book, *Koreatown*, had to offer a candid and uncompromised snapshot of what it's like to eat and drink in Korean American communities today. We didn't want to write a book narrated by a whispering woman dressed in silks, but a real-life look at the proudly industrious and sophisticated society hiding behind neon signage and heavy oak doors—doors many non-Koreans just walk by in cities and towns across the United States.

Our book would document how the rich food culture of Koreatown adheres to centuries of tradition traced back to Korea, yet is distinctly American. It would take you inside the kitchens and lives of the people who make their Koreatowns vibrant and delicious. And all this while showing how Korean food is inspiring chefs of all backgrounds are cooking today, articulated through recipes, stories and boots-on-the-ground photography.

So after over two years of travel, circling the United States from New York to Washington, D.C. to Atlanta, Chicago, San Francisco and Los Angeles, after count-less meals and conversations with the cooks, busi-ness owners and Korean American food obsessives, what did we figure out? Well, first, that you will never get sick of Korean food. But also that this food has a true spirit, and that spirit can be brought into your home kitchen with the recipes and techniques that follow. And if you also learn a little bit about Korean culture—or find yourself aboard the Seoul Train some late Friday night—even better.

So here we are. Recipes, stories, portraits of cooks and grocers and ice cream makers and a whole lot of soju: This is Koreatown.

## ABOUT THE BOOK'S PHOTOGRAPHY

The photos are shot primarily by the talented Sam Horine, with some fine contributions from Gabi Porter. The images were captured live, during our travels. Unlike most cookbooks, which are shot in air-conditioned studios using controlled lighting and methodical food styling, great efforts were made to do the exact opposite—to capture the food and people of Koreatown in their natural environment, in over 125 bars, markets, grocery stores and restaurants. The photos are not meant to simply show how a dish should look after following the directions.

With this documentary-style approach, some of the photos of the recipes are plated imprecisely. But they are meant to tell you a story and to give you the feel of these places: The smell of freshly poured sesame oil, the steam from a bubbling pot of kongbiji jjigae ris-ing up and warming your face. This time-consuming technique paid off greatly, which left Sam's camera splattered with ssamjang and the authors experienc-ing moments of extreme warmth, generosity, a few strange looks, and lots of stories.

# I HATE KOREATOWN.
# I LOVE KOREATOWN.

"I hate Koreatown." These are the words I hear whenever someone in my group of Korean friends suggests a night out. Then, it's almost like a script. "Why is Koreatown always so damn crowded?" "Why does the soju cost so much?" "Why so much MSG!?" Someone goes off about how ridiculous it would be to wait in line for food we believe (well, know) to be subpar to Chef Mom's version, and I say that even as a professional chef. This brings on talk of our respective mama's greatest culinary hits. Our throats begin to dry as the conversation briefly shifts to one-upping each other's most memorable drunken K-Town stories, like the Lob City locker room comparing their dunks on *Sportscenter*'s Top 10. Now the hunger starts to hit. We start making awkward eye contact with each other, and then we start hailing cabs to the corner of 32nd Street and Broadway, to the heart of New York City's Koreatown.

Ok, so we're a bunch of hypocritical bastards! But, when it comes down to it, there *are* reasons why my friends and I have such a love-hate relationship with the food in Koreatown. Sure, we all have a little bit of mama's boy in us. But also, a lot of the restaurants in Koreatown are small, family-run businesses—working in one of the most perilous, tiny-margin industries around. Cutting corners, for many of these places, is often a matter of survival, especially in the hyper-competitive real-estate market in Manhattan, the Koreatown I've known for most of my life.

Still, there is an untold number of incredibly exciting things happening in Koreatowns around the country—in Los Angeles, New York City, Atlanta, Minneapolis and more. Matt and I started working on this book to share our love of Korean and Korean American cooking, and the more we traveled and talked and ate in restaurants serving Korean communities, the more inspired we became. Time after time we found cooks who strive to do things the right way. To feed their guests well out of pride. We also found out how much American chefs, of many backgrounds, love Koreatown.

There was late-night barbecue and karaoke with Paul Qui and a pack of southern chefs in Duluth, Georgia. There was a deep conversation about jangs, staple condiments in the Korean kitchen, with the owners of a wonderful restaurant called Soban in Los Angeles. Unhappy with the quality of the products they found here, they did something about it, importing their own meju, the soybean base, to start making their own doenjang and gochujang. There was a night sitting at the counter of Serpico in Philadelphia, talking to my former chef, Peter, about his version of kimchi stew, which he finishes using drops of essential oils. And the night we searched for a near-mythic bossam restaurant in a driving rainstorm in a Northern Virginia suburb (we never did find it). And then there was the time I introduced Matt to the best bowl of gamjatang, a roaring pork and potato soup, prepared by a dutiful emo near where I grew up in New Jersey.

As we took in the stories of these cooks and business owners, my understanding of the Koreatown spirit grew deeper. And I realized that my own journey as a cook follows a similar path as many of these proud men and women, even if my stops along the way were different than those of most immigrant cooks.

I started cooking professionally at 15, and I've been blessed to graduate from a fancy culinary school, work in a three-Michelin-star kitchen and be mentored by some of the most influential chefs in the industry. But I returned to Koreatown—literally—to run my own kitchen at Kang Ho Dong Baekjeong, one of the busiest Korean restaurants in New York City. Something about this craft made me endure this masochistic, yet intensely gratifying, journey: There's something about conceptualizing a dish in your mind, creating it with your own hands and serving it to the people you love that is just still so raw and beautiful to me. Only recently, I realized the dishes that I most love cooking and sharing, the dishes I constantly think about, always have a connection to my heart . . . my Korean heart.

The pages of this book reflects the journey we have taken. Outside of a handful of guest contributions, these are the dishes and recipes I grew up on (both prepared at home and ordered in Koreatown), developed and tested in my small apartment kitchen and the home kitchens of our trusted friends and family, Koreans and non-Koreans. My goal with these recipes is to show people of all backgrounds how delicious and accessible this food is, even if many of the dishes might not be exactly what you find at your favorite Korean barbecue restaurant. But at the end of the day I want to give you the best—and that best is my bowl of kalbi jjim. Because I love Koreatown.

**BY DEUKI HONG**

# HOW A WHITE BOY JEW FROM KALAMAZOO
# FELL HARD FOR KOREAN FOOD

Jason Ough, the most stylish rock-band guitarist/ med-school student, shit-talking, Biggie-quoting, marathon-running Korean American best friend a guy could ever ask for, always did the ordering. Most of me loved that. Employed as a so-called food writer— as in, paid to interview chefs and sometimes sent bottles of cheap rum and out-of-state cupcakes from PR companies—I was the guy who had to know if the new Catalan joint in Chelsea was worth its salted cod, or if the new urban barbecue pit really tasted like the Hill Country. Friends, and sometimes strangers cc'd into my universe, leaned on me for advice. My off-hours sometimes felt like a job.

So I was always happy to let Jason take over for the night whenever we'd crowd around a table at Kum Gang San or Hanbat or one of his other favorite Koreatown spots in Manhattan. He'd speak to the server in short bursts of his parents' native tongue. It was the only time I'd ever hear him speak Korean, and it was impressive, especially after I realized he had just ordered several courses, often including scallion-squid pancakes and the extra-aged kimchi reserved only for only those who can locate Daegu on a map.

And though it was nice to shelve the pro foodie badge for an evening, when Jason ordered strips of well-marinated short ribs for the grill and a communal pot of chicken and ginseng soup that I would much later learn was called samgyetang, I secretly began to resent him for knowing so much about his native cuisine—and for not getting me with the program sooner.

For an article I was reporting, I recruited Jason and his wife to hike around Queens and Brooklyn to sample the city's best KFC (addictively crispy Korean fried chicken). In the wintertime, we would meet at Cho Dang Gol for spicy kalbi jjim and bowls of bubbling silken tofu. And then, in the summer of 2012, I received a short, cryptic e-mail that would change my relationship with Korean food forever.

It was written by a representative from the Korean Food Foundation, an arm of the Korean government that promotes the cuisine around the world. The representative—who I would later befriend and lovingly refer to as Nadia my K-Town fixer—was publishing a guidebook to the top Korean restaurants in New York City. She sought a journalist willing to visit seventy-five Korean restaurants anonymously and rate them. Naturally, I texted Jason right away:

"Jason! WTF. Is this real? You and I will be doing some recon."

Within weeks, I was signed on to lead the guidebook project. The assignment was unnerving. I, a white boy from western Michigan, would be required to visit five *dozen* different Korean restaurants. Could I handle the pressure of ordering? Could I eat that much ddeokbokki?

The project began on September 28, 2012, at an upscale vegetarian restaurant, Hangawi, and soon I was traveling all over the city. One night in Murray Hill, Queens, I felt like I had traveled to a quiet suburb of Seoul and settled in at a place called Han Joo Chik Naeng Myun & BBQ, where the specialty is samgyeopsal (pork belly), prepared on fancy crystal grills that are said to provide a superior char and health benefits (I can confirm the char, but am slightly skeptical about the health claim).

The dining room at Han Joo is well-worn and, much like the neighborhood, *transporting*. You will find only Koreans dining there. Korean medical dramas unfold on the glowing plasma screen. Korean newspapers pile up in a corner. But like most of the restaurants in Koreatown, there are no hard feelings toward outsiders. Everybody's there for the pork, and damn straight everybody's excited for the pork.

We dipped the glistening pig in a combination of sesame oil and salt, and then a soybean powder that adds an extra punch of earthiness. As tradition demanded, we ended the meal with a bowl of naengmyeon, cold buckwheat noodles served in a chilled broth of beef stock. A TV flickered overhead, playing the morning news in Seoul.

The evening at Han Joo was one of many moving food moments that took place during the visits, and I soon found myself a full-blown devotee of the cuisine and the culture. My wife, Tamar, liked to half joke that I was converting to Korean after returning from a long day of jokbal, kimbap and dakdoritang. I would text

Jason, complaining that the day's soondae was seasoned incorrectly. "Not the way umma makes it," even though I didn't actually have a Korean mother to call "umma."

As I wrapped up the guidebook, friends began to ask if I was sick of Korean food yet. But as my palate became more in touch with the funk, fire and straight-up awesomeness of the Korean kitchen, I started to crave the stuff. And, eventually, cook it at home.

Today, as I complete the research, writing and recipe testing for this book, I find myself eating in Koreatown, or making Korean food at home, two to three times a week. I'll walk into one of my favorite restaurants, Muk Eun Ji, with friends or fellow food writers, and I will say something to the server before we are seated. Banchan will arrive, starring a special extra-aged kimchi served only by request. Will it be jjampong or jajangmyeon, or maybe daeji kalbi with a side of kimchi bokkeumbap? The menu is in my hand. And now it's my duty to order for the table.

**BY MATT RODBARD**

# INGREDIENTS & EQUIPMENT
## THINGS YOU SHOULD FAMILIARIZE YOURSELF WITH.
## THINGS YOU SHOULD BUY.

If you're a little new to cooking Korean food, the first thing you'll want to do is load up on the key ingredients. But here's some good news: the Korean larder is relatively pared down compared with other food cultures in Asia, and many Korean dishes can be made using products that are already common to Western home cooks. These include garlic, ginger, scallions, soy sauce, sesame oil, tofu and, of course, kimchi. In this section, we wanted to help familiarize you with some products you might not know, as well as touch on some common items that are used slightly differently in Korean kitchens. This is by no means an exhaustive encyclopedia of all Korean food terms, but it'll get you where you need to go with all the recipes in this book. And if you're stuck on something, hit us up on Twitter (@deukihong and @mattrodbard). Try us!

---

### KOREAN MOTHER SAUCES: GOCHUJANG, DOENJANG AND GANJANG

Much of Korean cooking is based around three essential, easy-to-find foundations called jangs—each plays a role in creating the layers of flavors for which Korean cooking is famous. Here's our nickel jang tour:

**Gochujang (Spicy Fermented Pepper Paste)** Everybody has gone nuts for sriracha, but all we've gotta say is that sriracha had better watch its back for gochujang. Identified by its bright red container, gochujang (pronounced go-CHOO-jong) is a force in the Korean kitchen and used in soups, stews, sauces and barbecue marinades. It's savory, slightly funky (in the best way), a little sweet and can be hotter than the peppers grown at Satan's CSA. So pay attention to the pepper rating system on the packaging. The level 2 or 3 rating is typically our move.

Back in the day, gochujang was produced once a year, around the first day of spring. But with technological advancements and global demand, it's now pumped out of factories like ketchup. The process is relatively straightforward: meju, a cement-like block of dried and fermented soybeans, is mixed with hot pepper flakes, barley, sweet rice flour and salted water, then left out in the sun to ferment and mellow for thirty to ninety days. In Korea, where virtually all jangs are produced, gochujang is aged in large earthenware pots. When used straight, the flavor of gochujang can be a little too intense, so it's always mixed in with things like sesame oil, rice vinegar, garlic, ginger and soy sauce.

**Doenjang (Fermented Bean Paste)** If gochujang is the fireworks at the Fourth of July celebration, doenjang (pronounced DEN-jong) is the music that plays along in the background. It's fundamental to Korean cooking, deep and graceful but without the flash. To produce it, meju is rehydrated with salted water and left to ferment in the sun for many months. The liquid (ganjang, see right) is then separated to leave a thick, salty paste. This is doenjang, which is used in many aspects of the Korean kitchen. The most widely known use is as the backbone of the barbecue condiment Ssamjang (page 115).

Doenjang is also used in what is arguably Korea's most-popular stew, Doenjang Jjigae (page 170). Many have suggested that Korean doenjang and Japanese miso are interchangeable in cooking, which is simply not accurate. Miso is typically sweeter and much milder, while doenjang is intentionally in-your-face. Please, if you respect yourself and your fellow diners and your Korean friends, do not use miso in any of these recipes. "You can call it miso just like you call a girl a ho: that is, you can't," writes Los Angeles chef Roy Choi, wisely, about doenjang in his memoir, *L.A. Son*.

**Ganjang (Korean Soy Sauce)** As mentioned, ganjang (pronounced GAN-jong) is the liquefied by-product from the production of doenjang—or, essentially, what everybody knows as soy sauce. In Korean cooking, there are two main types available: regular and those used for soups. The regular variety is very similar to those varieties found in China and Japan: salty, earthy and packed with umami. The soup variety of soy sauce is unique to Korea. It is much lighter in color and sodium content and, as the name suggests, used in a variety of soup broths. It is also key when preparing namul (marinated vegetables). A good rule of thumb with soy sauce is to buy the low-sodium variety. Salt can always be added but never taken away.

**HERE ARE FEW MORE THINGS TO KEEP ON HAND WHEN COOKING WITH THIS BOOK.**

Ingredient and gear sections can be super boring in cookbooks! We tried to make this one less so. Read it and we promise you will learn something.

**Anchovies (Myeolchi)** Some anchovies are fishy, while others are mellow and briny, and all are sold in different sizes. They are used in many ways and add a natural reminder of the ocean, which plays a major role in Korean cooking. Anchovy Stock (page 195) is the base for many hot pots and requires a quality product. The

Making doenjang

Fermenting jangs

good stuff doesn't come cheap, imported from Busan and sold frozen for ten to fifteen dollars a box or small bag. The best anchovies have healthy, shiny skin and oftentimes are sold frozen; humidity is an anchovy's worst enemy, which is why you should keep them in the freezer.

**Black Bean Paste (Chunjang)** While similar to Chinese black bean sauce, many Korean cooks are emphatic that there is no substitution for this funky product. It's made from roasted soybeans and thus is nuttier and less salty than the Chinese version. Chunjang is the the main ingredient used in Jajangmyeon (page 97), a popular Korean-Chinese noodle dish.

**Chile Peppers (Gochu)** We use both green and red fresh chile peppers in this book, which are found at all Korean grocery stores. Korean green peppers are more vegetal than hot, closer to a bell pepper than a jalapeño. Thus they are often incorporated into dishes raw, or cooked lightly, as flavor enhancers. The long Korean red chile pepper offers more heat. It's also used raw but mostly dried and ground into gochugaru. If you need to substitute, try Anaheim peppers first and jalapeños next.

**Disposable Plastic Gloves** Buy a box for making kimchi and thank us later.

**Electric Rice Cooker** If you have the cupboard space and thirty bucks, an electric rice cooker is a wise investment. Nearly every Korean family has a rice cooker resting prominently in their kitchen. Most of the food cooked from this book is to be enjoyed with a bowl of rice. While we offer a very good stovetop method (page 73), nothing beats the set-it-and-forget-it convenience of a rice cooker. And if you find yourself flush, spend $200 and the thing will sing a K-pop song for you when the rice is ready.

**Fish Sauce (Aekjeot)** We use fish sauce, also referred to as anchovy sauce, in a few dishes. It's not as much a staple in Korean cooking as Thai or Vietnamese. But for all of our recipes, we highly recommend using the brand Red Boat. The producers use only anchovies and salt, and they make it the traditional way with no fillers. And you don't want to know what kind of filler is in some of the off-brand fish sauces you will find.

**Garlic (Maneul)** For those who have never shopped at an H Mart or any big Korean grocery store, a first trip to the produce section is a bit of a shocker. Good god is there a ton of garlic there! Peeled and unpeeled. Pickled and pulverized. It makes sense, as South Korea trails only China and India in annual garlic production, and once you've cooked anything at all in this book, you will see how nearly every dish calls for a clove or twelve. Selecting good garlic is as easy as

**Makgeolli**

grocery stores. Using a mix is a little funny, given that so much Korean food is made from scratch, but this pancake mix saves on time and is exactly what they use at restaurants—a blend of flour, baking powder and cornstarch that helps with both texture and flavor. We use the packaged pancake mix in our jeon recipes (pages 66–69).

**Kimchi** There's a wide generalization that kimchi is exclusively the fermented cabbage product you last found wedged atop a taco at your town's hip taqueria. While napa cabbage kimchi is one of the most popular types, other vegetables like daikon radish, cucumbers and green onions can be "kimchi'd." Yes, we think of *kimchi* as more of a verb than a noun. See page 39 for more about what we're talking about.

opening your eyes (make sure the bulb looks plump and healthy, not shrivelled) and nose (if you're buying garlic already peeled, give it a whiff—it should be full and not faded). And in a pinch, don't be afraid to buy garlic already minced in a jar. If you cook your way through this book, you're going to use it.

**Honey Powder** Many Koreans are skeptical about cooking with processed granulated sugar. Honey powder—sometimes called cactus honey powder—is one of the most popular alternatives. It's made from honey or sometimes agave, the same cactus that produces tequila. The flavor is less sweet than sugar, with a distinct honey-like quality. We use honey powder throughout the book in banchan, soups, meat marinades and desserts. It can also be used in hot coffee or tea.

**Jeon Mix** Crisp, savory pancakes (called jeon) are one of the most popular Korean foods, ordered at restaurants with particular glee. But here's a secret about those wonderful pancakes: they are almost always made from a mix, which you can find at all Korean

**Kimchi Refrigerator** These small refrigerators (think dorm-room size) are widely sold in Korea, as well as in appliance stores in the larger Koreatowns in the United States. If you are working on a crucial thirty-day kimchi fermentation, you don't necessarily want to be reminded about that every time you open the fridge door. If you plan on working through these recipes, have the space (like a garage or sub-basement) and want to tell your friends that you're getting serious about Korean food, pick one up. It can hold your soju supply too.

**Magic Bullet Food Processor** Manipulating large quantities of pulverized onions, radish, Asian pears, carrots and cabbage is a distinctly Korean kitchen move, so food processors are *great*. While Deuki is all cool with his hulking Vitamix—the Ferrari of the food processor world—we know that many are not so lucky. A good option is the Magic Bullet, which you can buy cheap on the Internet or in the As Seen On TV aisle at your local superstore. It's a great little gadget, sold with multiple detachable cups. You can designate one of them for your adventures in Korean cooking, so your next strawberry smoothie doesn't taste like kimchi. Paint a little Korean flag on it if you are into arts and crafts.

**Makgeolli** Makgeolli is Korea's oldest alcoholic beverage—a low-proof (around 6 percent alcohol by volume), unfiltered rice wine. Good makgeolli is slightly effervescent and has a pleasant mouthfeel, similar to skim milk (to the Western drinker it might sound a little weird to be describing an alcoholic beverage this way, but you're going to have to trust us a bit). Unfortunately, much of the makgeolli shipped to the United States is treated with preservatives to last the journey—it's tasty and gets the job done, but it's not makgeolli at its best. Paving the way here for the really good stuff is Slow City Makgeolli, a Chicago-based producer with growing distribution throughout the United States (see page 240).

**Mirin** Mirin is similar to Japanese sake, though with a very focused sweetness and made with a lower alcohol content. It's typically used in a braise or marinade to tenderize meat, and the alcohol eventually cooks off. Alternatively, Koreans use mihyan, a light and alcohol-free cooking wine that is less sweet and intense than mirin.

**Perilla (Kkaennip)** Similar to Japanese shiso, perilla is used prominently in the Korean kitchen to wrap meat or garnish soups and hot pots. Its flavor is vaguely mint-like with hints of citrus. Perilla is found at any good Korean grocery store and most Asian grocery stores. Substituting shiso or sesame leaf is OK too, but do not substitute with fresh mint.

**Radish (Mu)** What you will find in most Asian groceries is the almost ubiquitous daikon radish. Big, crisp and juicy, they are generally longer and thinner than the Korean bachelor or summer radish but are a fine

substitute for soups and stews. When making radish kimchi, though, it is best to seek out Korean radishes specifically, which have a milder, sweeter flavor.

**Red Chile Powder (Gochugaru)** Korean red chile powder is sold both coarsely and finely ground. The flavor is sweet and ever-so-slightly smoky, but the main function is to add heat. As you will find out, this food can be H-O-T. We're not going to say this often, but it's essential to buy gochugaru, as cayenne or crushed red pepper flakes will just not work the same. We've written all these recipes precisely for the flavor and heat level of gochugaru. Prices can range from a couple dollars to nearly twenty for the Merck-grade artisanal stuff. And watch out for the gochugaru made from finely ground seeds, which is where the dark heart of the heat lives. Matt once bought a small bag at Tongin Market in Seoul and cooked with it back in New York. That was not pretty.

**Rice (Bap)** Rice is central at the Korean table and served at basically every meal as either a side dish to accompany a sizzling sautéed dish or as the "glue" that binds together grilled meat and lettuce leaves. Rice can be served plain (ssalbap) or mixed together with barley (boribap) or millet (jobap). Koreans traditionally use short grain. Rice is so important in Korean culture that the popular greeting *Bap meogeosseoyo* translates to "Have you eaten rice today?"

**Rice Cakes (Dduk)** Koreans love rice cakes—rice flour combined with boiling water and salt and pounded into a dough, which is then set and cut into a variety of shapes for different dishes. They can be slices, cylinders or batons, and they have a unique texture— tougher and chewier than an Italian noodle—and are great at absorbing flavor. Rice cakes are always best when bought freshly made that day, which you can find at most Korean grocery stores or markets—namely,

the tube-shaped variety used in the popular dish ddeokbokki. You can also find rice cakes refrigerated or dried, which must be boiled beforehand. Rice cakes are a fixture of the Korean kitchen and consumed in quantities that are unrivaled by the Chinese, Japanese and basically any country on the planet.

**Rice Vinegar** This important acid is milder than Western vinegars and you can find it at any supermarket or health food store. And make sure not to substitute white or balsamic vinegar in any of these recipes, as they have very different flavors and acidity levels and won't translate. We like to use rice vinegar to cut through doenjang or gochujang in dipping sauces and meat marinades.

**Sake** Sake, the Japanese rice wine of sushi bar and "bomb" fame, is used in a few of our meat marinade recipes. The alcohol masks some of the more extreme "beefy" and "porky" elements that some Koreans don't necessarily like that much (while others adore it), but it also aids in tenderizing. When buying sake for cooking, the dry kind is best. And, of course, don't spend too much money on the bottle, because it's going up in smoke anyway.

**Salted Shrimp (Saeujeot)** Salted shrimp is what it sounds like—salted baby shrimp (OK, it's fermented too). It smells, honestly, like something you would toss in the aquarium but is an essential ingredient in kimchi recipes, and when cooked or blended, its flavor mellows. Not to be confused with dried shrimp, salted shrimp is sold in small jars and found in the refrigerator in all Asian grocery stores.

**Seaweed (Gim)** The names can be a bit confusing, but in general, *laver* (English) = *nori* (Japanese) = *gim* (Korean). Koreans pride themselves on the seaweed farmed in the pristine waters off the country's southwest coast, and it comes in many forms. You are probably familiar with the small packages of roasted and seasoned seaweed that are sold at health food stores and Trader Joe's. That's one popular type of seaweed. We use it in a few noodle and rice bowl recipes, sheared with scissors for a tasty garnish. Miyeok (also called wakame) is another type of seaweed, silky smooth when rehydrated in liquid and used in a birthday soup called Miyeokguk (page 194). Dashima (known widely by its Japanese name, kombu) is used mostly in stocks. Dashima is sold in fossilized sheets, and a little goes a long way. The takeaway from eating and cooking with seaweed? *Do it*. Its flavor is between that of a garden vegetable and a raw oyster. It's so unique it's almost impossible not to love. It's impossibly healthy too.

**Sesame Oil (Chamgireum)** Some have called sesame oil the olive oil of Asia, which is on the right track. In Korea, high-quality sesame oil is valued so dearly that some will source their own sesame seeds, toast them to their specifications and take the seeds to a mill for processing. In Koreatowns in America, sesame oil dealers are neighborhood fixtures—and sometimes secretive. A *Los Angeles Times* writer was once chased out of a shop when she started to take a photo. The reason for all this effort is that once you've tasted a freshly pressed product, drizzled over a bowl of rice or painted on a hunk of kalbi, there's no way in hell you are going back. The best bet is to buy a couple bottles from the Asian grocery store and see which one you like (some are "nuttier" while others tend to be "sweeter," and calling one the best comes down to a matter of taste). And unless you are cooking at home a ton, it's best to buy sesame oil in small quantities and keep it refrigerated, as it can go rancid.

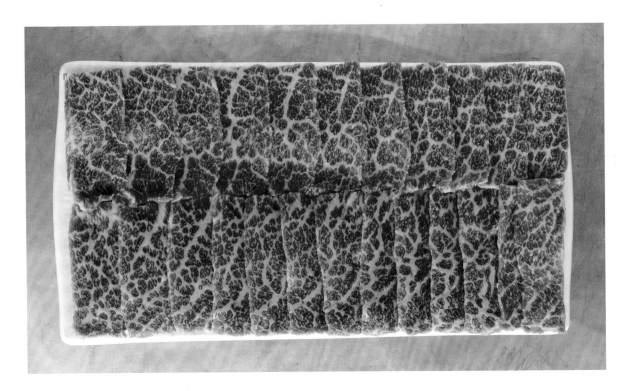

**Sesame Seeds** Good roasted sesame seeds should taste nutty. Bad (old, stale, turned) sesame seeds taste less nutty. You want nutty because nutty is the essence you are going for, not just texture or a pretty garnish for Instagram. If that container of seeds has been sitting in the back of your pantry for five years, chances are they are in the less nutty category.

**Syrups (Mulyeot)** The use of syrups is Korean cooking is widespread, and there are many. Mulyeot is clear and made from corn, while darker ssalyeot is made from rice, both available at any Korean grocery. (Syrups made with barley and plums are also available.) Mulyeot and the many derivatives are lighter and slightly less processed. In a pinch you can also substitute honey, though you may want to cut back on the amount, as honey is sweeter and more floral.

**Soju** Soju is the national drink of Korea, where it is cheaper than bottled water. It tastes like a sweeter, milder vodka and can be mixed with basically any-thing. Generally speaking, it's a clear beverage distilled from rice, barley, wheat or sweet potatoes. The alcohol content starts at about 15 percent and can go up to 45 percent with more premium bottles. In some states, soju is covered under a restaurant's beer and wine license, even though it is considerably more powerful than beer and wine, creating a subgenre of soju-based cocktails (that, to be honest, often taste pretty terrible). Also, soju is often confused with shochu, a higher-proof and generally more refined distilled beverage found commonly in Japan.

**Stone Bowls (Ddukbaegi)** Investing in a set of heat-proof stone bowls is money well spent. They are great for both serving up bubbling-hot stews (jjigae) and for cooking directly on the stove—easy to clean and holding heat extremely well (almost too well, as those who have burnt themselves an hour after the meal was served can recall). Koreans are famous for technological innovation (see that Samsung phone in your pocket), but this is the ultimate lo-fi equipment.

**Tabletop Barbecue Grill** So you know that thing where you grill your own meat on the table at a Korean barbecue restaurant? That's fun, right? Well, you can do it at home if you buy one of these for like forty dollars. The propane model is the best, as electrics don't have the proper juice for high-temp grilling.

**Tofu (Dubu)** The ubiquitous bean curd foodstuff you know as tofu is called dubu in Korea, but for the sake of confusement, we call it tofu in the recipes. There are many kinds of tofu available in both Asian markets and supermarkets, and in the recipes we specify what type is needed. For Soondubu Jjigae (page 173), it's the extra-silken variety, while firmer tofu is used in fried and braised dishes, as well as Tyler Kord's incredible submarine sandwich (page 218). While we don't side with a specific brand, it's always best to use the fresh stuff whenever possible. You can sometimes find freshly pressed tofu in Korean-owned markets or convenience stores. And if the Korean restaurant you are eating at makes their own, which is sometimes advertised proudly on signage, you are in for a treat.

**Yakult Probiotic Yogurt Drink** If you've ever dined at a Korean barbecue restaurant, chances are you've encountered this meal-closing tradition. Koreans aren't super big on desserts, so a shot of this half-sweet, half-tart yogurt-like substance is the next best thing. The mixture is glugged down to aid in digestion (there's a special strain of good bacteria in there as well, at least that's what the advertisement says).

## SO, WHERE CAN I SHOP FOR ALL THIS GREAT STUFF?

As mentioned, there are many ingredients that can be found at your standard grocery store. Many towns are home to both large Korean chains like H Mart and smaller, family-run grocery stores that carry the important jangs, frozen anchovies shipped straight from Busan and dried seaweed. Matt's parents live in Kalamazoo, Michigan—located in the state's southwestern corner and home to a small Asian population—and they have a small Korean grocery store stocked with everything needed to cook from this book.

As a last resort, there are a number of online resources. Also, when you are bored at work, shopping on the Internet cannot be avoided sometimes. Here are a few sites to get lost in:

**CrazyKoreanShopping.com** An extension of the smart K-food blog *Crazy Korean Cooking*, this web-only store is a good place to find both necessary kitchen staples and equipment and a few quirky offerings—all with clearly written descriptions, which is a big plus.

**AsianFoodGrocer.com** A massive selection of both shelf-stable and perishable foods, equipment and energy drinks are available here. The noodle section alone is worth a spin.

**Kalustyans.com** This specialty store located in New York City sells over 4,000 specialty spices, herbs and teas and is a favorite of local chefs.

# GUIDE TO KOREAN PRODUCE

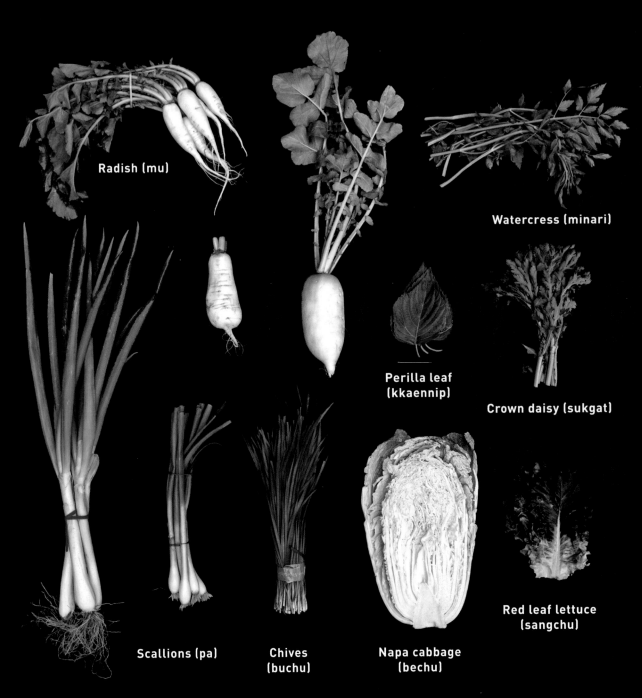

Radish (mu)

Watercress (minari)

Perilla leaf
(kkaennip)

Crown daisy (sukgat)

Red leaf lettuce
(sangchu)

Scallions (pa)

Chives
(buchu)

Napa cabbage
(bechu)

Green onions
(daepa)

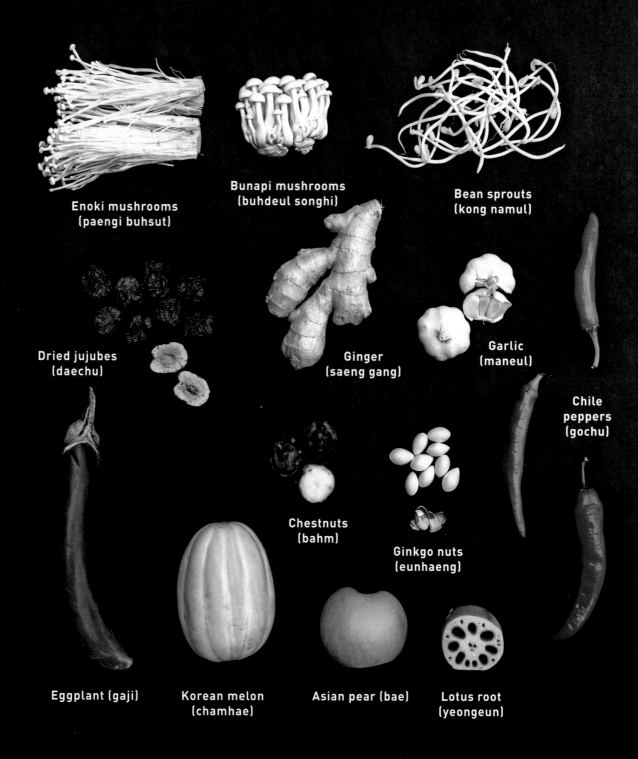

**Enoki mushrooms
(paengi buhsut)**

**Bunapi mushrooms
(buhdeul songhi)**

**Bean sprouts
(kong namul)**

**Dried jujubes
(daechu)**

**Ginger
(saeng gang)**

**Garlic
(maneul)**

**Chile
peppers
(gochu)**

**Chestnuts
(bahm)**

**Ginkgo nuts
(eunhaeng)**

**Eggplant (gaji)**

**Korean melon
(chamhae)**

**Asian pear (bae)**

**Lotus root
(yeongeun)**

# Kimchi & Banchan

김치 & 반찬

They say that Korean restaurants should be judged by the quality of their banchan, the various small plates that land on the table to mark the beginning of a Korean meal. They also say that a restaurant should be judged by the pace at which they are refilled by the servers (almost always free of charge, included in the price of the entrees). By these measures, Soban—a small restaurant located on the western edge of L.A.'s sprawling Koreatown—may be the best Korean restaurant in America.

The restaurant is run by a husband-and-wife couple from Jeolla-do, long considered Korea's breadbasket. The region is also known for exceptional banchan, and a visit to the homey little spot is a small-plate tour de force. Custardy steamed egg, tofu both silky fresh and braised in soy sauce, lotus root, eggplant, a small fried croaker and kimchis of various stages of funk and fire. All plunked onto the table with frenetic *thwacks*.

The literal translation for banchan is "side dish," but banchan should be thought of as an essential part of the meal, to be eaten in concert with the main courses. You can walk into any Korean restaurant, of any style, price or quality level, and you're going to be presented with banchan. Kimchi is, of course, the most well-known banchan. Seasoned vegetables, called muchim, are also a type of banchan, tossed with a combination of sesame oil, soy sauce, sugar and gochugaru.

Banchan is also a big part of the Korean home kitchen and prepared in seconds by simply dressing vegetables—or over the course of weeks or months in the case of fermenting kimchi.

In this chapter we've included recipes that span the small-plates spectrum, from our go-to kimchis to quick pickles to more elaborate dishes like marinated crab. We've also included pancakes in this chapter, which aren't typically part of the banchan taxonomy, but hell if we weren't going to bring those up early. Korean pancakes are the best. 쁘

# KOREAN SMALL PLATES & SIDE DISHES

Banchan arrives at the table in many shapes, sizes and quantities, all meant to serve as a complement to the main course—a large cauldron of soup, a platter of braised meat or something sizzling from the barbecue grill. We often get asked which side dish goes with what, and we always like to answer simply that there are no rules with banchan. If you want to corner the plate of radish kimchi and eat it straight, go for it. If you want to spoon some braised tofu and dip it into a steaming bowl of doenjang jjigae, go for it. Potato salad and grilled short ribs, wrapped in a pickled daikon radish disk and drizzled with a little sesame oil? *Yes.* When were were photographing this book, we spent an afternoon at the great Park's Barbeque in Los Angeles. We asked owner Jenee Kim to bring out a few of the dishes she likes on the side. This is what she put on the table, a spread for the ages available on any given night at a Koreatown near you.

**FIRST ROW (LEFT TO RIGHT):** Fish cake and cucumber salad, crunchy sesame bean sprouts (page 51), soy-braised beef and mushrooms, wok-fried glass noodles (page 84), soy-marinated tofu

**SECOND ROW:** Fried squash, dried daikon radish muchim (page 53), soy-marinated raw beef (page 152), bubbling egg (page 62), spicy marinated crab (page 64)

**THIRD ROW:** Acorn jelly, radish quick kimchi (page 40), soy-marinated eggplant (page 52), cucumber quick kimchi (page 39), egg and seafood omelet

**FOURTH ROW:** Napa cabbage kimchi (page 41), spring onion quick kimchi (page 40), tofu and spinach, peppers with dried anchovies (page 54), daikon wraps (page 47)

# Five Quick Kimchis to Keep in Your Fridge. Always.

## 김치

A common perception is that kimchi refers to the spicy pickled cabbage you find anywhere grape jelly, Coke Zero and sriracha are sold, which is basically every store these days. Indeed, napa cabbage kimchi is one of the most popular types, and you will find our recipe on page 41. But really, kimchi is simply a pickling *technique,* not a single item. Many things, like cucumbers, chives and apples, can also be kimchi'd. The recipe we offer here is a good place to start; it's a flavorful kimchi base that can be used to pickle a wide variety of fruits and vegetables, though five in particular pop into our heads.

## MAKE THE KIMCHI MARINADE

This is what gives the kimchi its guts: a blend of sweetness, heat and brininess. Using a quality fish sauce is important, so we prefer to spend a little bit extra on a smaller-batch Vietnamese brand called Red Boat. **MAKES ENOUGH MARINADE FOR 1 POUND OF VEGETABLES**

**½ cup peeled, cored and chopped Asian pear**

**½ cup coarsely ground gochugaru**

**¼ cup fish sauce**

**2 garlic cloves, minced**

**2 tablespoons sugar**

**2 teaspoons minced ginger**

Add the pear, gochugaru, fish sauce, garlic, sugar and ginger to a food processor and run until smooth.

## MAKE THE CURE MIX

This simple cure is used to draw out extra liquid and add additional seasoning. **MAKES 6 TABLESPOONS**

**3 tablespoons sugar**

**3 tablespoons kosher salt**

In a small bowl, stir together the sugar and salt. **NOW YOU ARE READY TO KIMCHI!**

### PERSIAN CUCUMBERS

Persian cucumbers are easily found and incredibly refreshing, which is why they're a banchan fixture. You can also substitute kirby or English varieties; just make sure you drain the excess liquid before adding the Kimchi Marinade.

**1 pound Persian cucumbers, sliced ¼ inch thick**

In a large pickling jar or lidded container, combine the cucumber and 1 tablespoon of the Cure Mix; let sit 15 minutes. Drain the excess liquid, then add 1 cup of the Kimchi Marinade, stirring to coat. Refrigerate for at least 2 hours. This kimchi will keep up to 1 week, refrigerated.

(recipes continue)

## DAIKON RADISH

Daikon radish is another common kimchi, which soaks up the marinade phenomenally well and remains addictively crisp for a few days.

**4 pounds daikon radish, trimmed, peeled and cut into 1-inch cubes**

In a large pickling jar or lidded container, combine the daikon and 4 tablespoons of the Cure Mix; let sit 15 minutes. Drain the excess liquid, then add 1 cup of the Kimchi Marinade, stirring to coat. Refrigerate for at least 2 hours. This kimchi will keep up to 2 weeks, refrigerated, but is at its crispest within a few days.

## GARLIC CHIVE OR SPRING ONION

One of our all time favorites is garlic chives, which are different than regular chives and can be found at most Asian grocery stores. Garlic chives are longer and have flatter leaves. The flavor is more mild and slightly sweet. You can also use spring onions or—hell we're going to say it—ramps.

**1 pound garlic chives or spring onions, cut into 2-inch batons**

In a large pickling jar or lidded container, combine the chives and 1 cup of the Kimchi Marinade. Refrigerate for 1 day. This kimchi will keep up to 2 weeks, refrigerated.

## BOK CHOY

Bok choy is a nice substitution for napa cabbage. It's neutral and absorbs the Kimchi Marinade really well while preserving a bit of crunch. It also looks really cool in the jar and on the plate.

**1 pound baby bok choy, washed thoroughly, trimmed and cut in half**

In a large pickling jar or lidded container, combine the baby bok choy and 2 tablespoons of the Cure Mix; let sit 15 minutes. Drain the excess liquid, then add 1 cup of the Kimchi Marinade, stirring to coat. Refrigerate for 2 days. This kimchi will keep 1 week, refrigerated.

## PINEAPPLE

Pineapple is our own invention, and we just have to pat ourselves on the back a little bit for it. When we first made it in the test kitchen, we couldn't stop eating it—with all its sweetness and acid and spice and tang and funk. It goes incredibly well with grilled meat, on a taco or with a bowl of ramyun. And in general, if you have any leftover marinade, dig through your refrigerator to see what else can be kimchi'd.

**1 large pineapple, trimmed, peeled and cut into 1-inch cubes**

In a large pickling jar or lidded container, combine the pineapple and 1 cup of the Kimchi Marinade, stirring to coat. Refrigerate for at least 2 hours. This kimchi will keep up to 1 week, refrigerated—but honestly, it's not going to last that long.

# Baechu Kimchi
## 배추김치
### NAPA CABBAGE KIMCHI

Napa cabbage: The granddaddy of all kimchi. This is the kimchi that people think of when they hear the word *kimchi*—from taco topper to the cooler case at Ralph's. There are literally thousands of different kimchi recipes and combinations, tied to the seasons. That said, this recipe is special.

Traditionally, napa kimchi is made in the late autumn (October through December) to prepare for the famously harsh Korean winter. The tradition is called kimjang, and back in the day entire communities got together to make it in large batches. We're talking as much as 100 heads of cabbage at at time, with recipes passed down village to village, generation to generation. But you can certainly make yourself a batch any time during the year if you can find plump and healthy napa cabbage.

**BUYING THE CABBAGE** Look for cabbage that appears healthy and fresh; remove the outer few layers of leaves if anything is browned. At Korean markets, the peeling away of blighted leaves is often done right in the store. The remaining leaves should be tightly packed.

**THE PASTE AND MARINADE** Next make the rice flour paste (an important binder) and the marinade, which includes an essential ingredient: salted fermented shrimp called saeujeot. While many recipes call for fish sauce, we feel the salted shrimp add a pronounced flavor that is just too good to omit. Once combined with the cabbage (don't forget to wear gloves!) and stuffed into glass jars or plastic containers of varying sizes, the waiting game begins.

(recipe continues)

FOR THE CABBAGE

12 cups water

1 cup coarse sea salt

1 large napa cabbage
(2 to 3 pounds)

FOR THE RICE FLOUR
PASTE

2 tablespoons sweet
rice flour

1 cup water

FOR THE MARINADE

1 small onion, roughly
chopped

½ cup roughly chopped,
peeled Asian pear

2-inch knob of ginger,
roughly chopped

6 garlic cloves, minced

4 Korean red chile
peppers, trimmed and
cut in half

¼ cup water

½ cup salted fermented
shrimp

¼ cup sugar

½ cup rice flour paste

1 cup coarsely ground
gochugaru

1 bunch scallions, green
parts only, thinly sliced

1 carrot, grated

½ cup peeled and grated
daikon radish

KIMCHI IS ALIVE AND ALWAYS CHANGING Kimchi is all about personal taste, and some like their kimchi fresh, while others like it older and funkier. Our general suggestion is to make a large batch (like 6 to 8 heads) and store it in several jars to sample after different time periods. But if you're new to the kimchi making process, start small with the recipe here and scale up later. After 5 days, pull out a small jar and eat it wrapped in lettuce with a hunk of grilled Kalbi (page 112). After 10 days, pull another jar and place on the table with Godeungeo Gui (broiled mackerel, page 128). Keep one in the back of your refrigerator for two months and stew it down in a Kimchi Jjigae (page 169). Or, at any age, just snack on it directly from the jar. Give a jar to your best friend or boss or favorite food fan. This is a serious stocking stuffer. **MAKES ABOUT 2 QUARTS**

1 **BRINE THE CABBAGE:** In a large container, combine 12 cups of cold water and the sea salt. Cut the napa cabbage head lengthwise, then into quarters. Place in the salt water and brine for 6 hours at room temperature. The brining step both adds flavor and opens the cabbage's pores, allowing the marinade to soak in. Rinse in cold water and have a little bite. If you would prefer it saltier, brine for another 6 hours to overnight; it's a matter of personal preference.

2 **MAKE THE RICE FLOUR PASTE:** Once the cabbage is brined, make the rice flour paste. In a small saucepan over medium-high heat, continually whisk the sweet rice flour and 1 cup water until it reaches a boil. Keep whisking for 2 minutes until it reaches a pudding-like consistency. Remove from heat, transfer to a container and refrigerate until cool.

3 **MAKE THE MARINADE:** Combine the onion, Asian pear, ginger, garlic, chile peppers and ¼ cup water in a food processor and run until smooth, then transfer to a large bowl. Add the shrimp, sugar, rice flour paste, gochugaru, scallion greens, carrot and daikon and combine well.

4 Drain the brined cabbage, rinse each piece well in cold water and place them in a very large bowl. While wearing plastic gloves, toss the cabbage with the marinade, coating well. Transfer to clean, large glass jars or clean plastic containers with lids that fit snugly. You can cut the cabbage to fit if you want, or keep the leaves whole and pack them tightly in the jars. Affix the lids, though not too tightly, and place the jars in a cool, dark and dry space and allow to ferment for 1 day. Heads up: The fermentation process may cause some kimchi juice to bubble over, so place the jars in a plastic bag. When done, refriger-

ate for 5 to 7 days, or until the kimchi has reached your desired level of funk. It will keep up to a month in the refrigerator to enjoy eaten directly from the container, or longer for use in further cooking, like in Kimchi Jeon (page 66) and Kimchi Jjigae (see page 169).

### SO HERE'S THE DEAL WITH UMAMI

You've likely heard about umami, the "fifth taste" coined in 1908 by Japanese scientist Kikunae Ikeda. We mention it often because the concept is critical to understanding the Korean kitchen. Basically, it's the taste that isn't sweet, salty, sour or bitter, but it is the deep, all-enveloping savory meatiness you find in, well, meats, mushrooms and many of the staples of Asian pantries. Things like fish sauce, doenjang, kombu, bonito flakes, anchovies, soy sauce and, especially, many kimchis are the source of an intergalactic war's worth of umami bombs. Mediterranean kitchen staples like aged cheese (hello, Parmigiano-Reggiano!) and tomatoes are also rich in umami.

So, what does this all mean for you while you visit your favorite local Korean restaurant or cook through the recipes in this book? It means that when a sudden, unrelenting craving for kongbiji jjigae or kimchi pajeon pops into your brain, it's nothing to fear. That's just the umami talking.

# Dongchimi
## 동치미
### WATER RADISH KIMCHI

There is a restaurant in Los Angeles called the Corner Place that takes the secrecy of their dongchimi recipe so seriously that they do not allow takeout. Ever. No exceptions. It makes sense, because when you nail the recipe (which they have, and we think we have as well), there is nothing more irresistibly refreshing. Dongchimi is a short-fermented radish kimchi traditionally served in the winter months—paired with steaming hot dishes—though you can often find it at restaurants year-round. Unlike the spicy red kimchis, dongchimi is a white "water kimchi." The pickling liquid is more of a broth and is slurped up with the tender radish. It's wonderful—sour but without an overpowering pop, a little sweet and spicy.

When buying the radishes for this kimchi, it's important to distinguish between Japanese (daikon) and Korean (mu) varieties. Japanese daikon is longer, thinner and slightly sweeter—and likely what you will find at your usual grocery stores. Korean radish is shorter and rounder and contains more water. A good Korean radish has a distinctive crunch and strong vegetable flavor, which is smoothed out after a couple days in the liquid, and they are strongly preferred for this. The kimchi will be ready in a week or so, depending on the season, and will keep for several months, evolving in flavor over time.

A favorite, simple dish you can also make from this is dongchimi guksu, a refreshing cold noodle. Boil white wheat somen noodles, drain and shock the noodles in cold water and serve them in a bowl with dongchimi and its liquid poured on top as a soup. Garnish with cucumber, scallions, tomato and chile pepper slices. MAKES 4 POUNDS KIMCHI, PLUS BRINE

1 In a large airtight container, combine radish and cabbage with the sugar and sea salt. Allow to sit, covered, at room temperature for 24 hours.

(recipe continues)

4 pounds Korean radish, peeled and cut into quarters

1 head of napa cabbage, quartered

4 tablespoons sugar

10 tablespoons coarse sea salt

1 onion, quartered

1 red apple, peeled, cored and quartered

1 Asian pear, peeled, cored and quartered

12 garlic cloves

2-inch knob of ginger

1 bunch scallions, trimmed

18 cups water

4 long, hot red chile peppers, thinly sliced with seeds removed

1 12-ounce can of lemon-lime soda

**2** The next day, the daikon and cabbage should have released a good amount of liquid. Do not strain this liquid; it's important in the fermentation process.

**3** Add the onion, apple, pear, garlic, ginger, scallions, chile peppers and 18 cups of water, making sure the vegetables are fully submerged. Seal tightly with the lid and let sit at room temperature for 3 to 5 days (in the summer) or closer to a week during cooler weather. Check on it and taste it daily; it should taste a little soured with some nice depth, which will grow the longer it ages.

**4** When the kimchi is to your liking, season the dongchimi liquid with the soda to add a refreshing sweetness. It should have a good balance of "funk" from the fermentation and a good spice kick from the chile peppers. Refrigerated, dongchimi keeps for several months. Serve ice cold, adding ice cubes if needed.

# Mu Ssam
## 무초절임
### DAIKON WRAP

Lightly pickled daikon radish wraps are one of the best complements for hunks of grilled marinated meat, offering a bright contrast and a refreshing way to wrap everything up in one bite. We like to pickle our own using an unconventional brine of lime, vinegar and beet juice, which turns the radish a gorgeous shade of red. You should seek out a Korean radish, as its mild, sweet flavor is excellent, but substitute with daikon as a last resort. **MAKES 1 POUND**

**1** Peel and thinly slice the radish, ideally using a mandoline slicer to get it paper-thin, and place the slices in a large bowl.

**2** In a large pot, combine the beet and lime juices, sugar, vinegar, sea salt and 6 cups of water. Set the pot over medium heat, stirring until the sugar dissolves, then remove it from the heat. Make sure not to boil the pickling liquid as it will lose acidity and color.

**3** Pour the pickling liquid over the radish slices, stir to make sure all the slices are coated in the brine and refrigerate for a minimum of 2 hours. Keep refrigerated; they will last for 1 week but have the best flavor when served within 2 days.

**1 Korean radish or daikon**

**½ pound beets, juiced**

**½ pound limes, juiced**

**6 cups water**

**2 cups sugar**

**1 cup Korean apple vinegar or white vinegar**

**¼ cup fine sea salt**

**Kosher salt to taste**

**1 pound baby spinach**

**1 tablespoon soy sauce**

**1 tablespoon sesame oil**

**1 teaspoon sugar**

**½ teaspoon black pepper**

**1 garlic clove, minced**

**1 teaspoon toasted sesame seeds, for garnish**

# Sigeumchi Muchim
## 시금치 무침
### SOY AND SESAME SPINACH

In Korean, muchim means to "mix with seasonings," and this is one of our favorites. We're confident Korean parents don't have to harp on their kids to eat their spinach, since the freshness of spinach pairs so well with earthy sesame oil, soy sauce and a touch of sugar. This recipe is really easy to make, can be served cold or at room temperature and is a great way to get the taste buds moving before the main event lands on the dinner table. This is why you will find this dish as part of most banchan spreads. **SERVES 4 TO 6**

1  Bring a large pot of water to a boil over high heat. Fill a bowl with ice water and set it nearby. Salt the pot generously, then blanch spinach in it for 30 seconds, until tender. Drain the spinach and shock it immediately in the ice-water bath. Drain again and squeeze the spinach to get rid of any excess water.

2  In a bowl, stir together the soy sauce, sesame oil, sugar, pepper and garlic. Add the spinach and toss thoroughly. Garnish with sesame seeds.

# Jangajji
## 장아찌

### QUICK SOY SAUCE PICKLES: DAIKON AND GARLIC, JALAPEÑO AND ONION, EGG

**PICKLING BASE**

**½ cup sugar**

**½ cup soy sauce**

**¾ cup rice vinegar**

Like kimchi, soy sauce pickles are a popular banchan. Here are three of our favorite versions, but they all use the same simple pickling liquid and can be made in about five minutes. Daikon and garlic, vegetal and astringent, are tamed by the pickling base. You might just shock yourself by snacking on a whole garlic clove (there's a reason you will find bottles of Scope in the bathrooms of Korean restaurants). Pickled jalapeños are a strictly North American affair and are big-time crowd-pleasers. Those go great with grilled Kalbi (page 112) but also on top of sandwiches and burgers. And soy-pickled eggs? Try keeping those around for a few days. They will not last. **SERVES 4**

Combine sugar, soy sauce and vinegar in a small pot and bring to a boil. Turn off heat and allow to cool for 15 minutes.

### DAIKON AND GARLIC

Pour the pickling base over **½ pound daikon** (peeled and cut into ½-inch cubes) and **8 whole garlic cloves** (peeled). Refrigerate for at least 4 hours. This will keep 1 week, refrigerated.

### JALAPEÑO AND ONION

Pour pickling base over **8 jalapeños** (sliced into ¼-inch rings) and **1 medium onion** (cut into large dice). Refrigerate for at least 4 hours. This will keep 1 week, refrigerated.

### EGG

Bring a pot of water to a boil and carefully lower in **6 eggs**. Boil for 7 minutes. Meanwhile, fill a large bowl with ice water. Remove the eggs and shock them in the ice water, then peel and place in a bowl. Pour the pickling base over the eggs, a **1-inch knob of ginger** (sliced into 3 pieces) and **1 Korean red chile** (halved). Refrigerate for at least 4 hours. These will keep 4 days, refrigerated.

# EATING KOREATOWN
## NOVELIST ADAM JOHNSON

"It was so hard to get to North Korea," says Adam Johnson of his 2007 research trip for his break-through novel, *The Orphan Master's Son*, winner of the 2013 Pulitzer Prize for Fiction. Johnson's children burst through the doors and into the smoke-and-sesame-oil air of Brothers Barbecue in San Francisco. The author towers over all of us, smiling, while the waitstaff set up our table—which soon will be piled with banchan and a house-made doenjang. Korean barbecue is now a weekly family tradition.

A cultural deep-dig swirled into page-turning narra-tive, his novel has been praised as an authentic por-trayal of life in the Hermit Kingdom. Johnson admits that depicting workaday North Korean life was nearly impossible with government censors controlling all communication. For the author, writing the book required years of research, including interviews with former residents and a highly monitored trip fixed through an NGO in China. In a country long plagued with mass starvation, food plays an essential role in

Johnson's story. "They remember the food nostalgi-cally and in great detail, family meals that they would never have again," he says.

When asked to size up his time with the food in North Korea, Johnson takes a measured approach. "They are going to take you to where they are going to take you, and you have zero say in the matter," he says, adding that besides the "absolutely fantastic" yuk-gaejang in Pyongyang, most of the food was bad to unsafe. "I must have shot ten-grand worth of antibi-otics to kill it," he says of the parasite he was gifted by Kim Jong Il. "They would always give us five times more food than we needed and make a point of show-ing us that they were throwing away the extras, to somehow prove that it all was plentiful." We wrap up with sikhye, a sweet rice drink.

"When you taste Korean food, you can taste the resil-ience of the people. It's food that is going to last the winter, or last the next invasion."

# Kongnamul Muchim

## 콩나물무침

### CRUNCHY SESAME BEAN SPROUTS

Stir-fried bean sprouts are a fixture of the banchan spread, and for good reason: they're a fresh, crunchy snack that merges sweetness, saltiness, the clean flavor of the sprouts and a distinctive note of sesame oil. The key here is making sure the bean sprouts are not overcooked so that they keep their crunch. We like to kick the heat up a bit with chiles, but you can, of course, adjust that for your own taste. SERVES 4

1  Heat sesame oil in a wok or large sauté pan over high heat. Add the garlic and sauté for 20 seconds, until very fragrant but still a shade of white.

2  Add the chile, bean sprouts, oyster sauce, sugar and scallion and sauté for about 2 minutes, tossing frequently; you are wilting the bean sprouts, but keep them a little crunchy. Season with salt and pepper to taste. This can be served warm, at room temperature or cold. It will keep in the refrigerator for a week.

**2 tablespoons sesame oil**

**2 garlic cloves, minced**

**1 red chile, sliced, with seeds**

**4 cups bean sprouts**

**2 tablespoons oyster sauce**

**2 teaspoons sugar**

**1 scallion, sliced**

**Salt and black pepper to taste**

2 medium Asian eggplants

1 tablespoon salt

1 tablespoon sugar

1 scallion, thinly sliced

1 Korean red chile pepper, seeded and thinly sliced

2 garlic cloves, minced

1 tablespoon soy sauce

1 tablespoon sesame seeds

1 tablespoon sesame oil

1 teaspoon black pepper

# Gaji Muchim
## 가지무침
### SOY-MARINATED EGGPLANT

This muchim is so easy to make, and it can work as a traditional banchan or a warm vegetable side dish to pair easily with basically anything. The sweetness from the sugar works well with the soy sauce and sesame oil. We love cooking with long, slender Asian eggplant for its versatility, meaty texture and ability to retain flavor. In this cookbook we mostly avoid the microwave but find it really makes for a tender, greaseless result here, and it's how Deuki grew up making it. You can make it on the stovetop as well. SERVES 4 TO 6

1  Cut the eggplants into ½ × 2-inch batons, about the size of a finger. Add salt and sugar and let sit for 20 minutes so the eggplants release their liquid, which you should drain.

2  Place the eggplants in a microwave-safe container and microwave on High for 2½ minutes. Toss and cook again for an additional 2½ minutes. The eggplant should turn a light brown color and soften slightly. (To use the stovetop, heat 1 tablespoon of vegetable oil in a large skillet over medium heat until shimmering. Add the eggplant and cook, tossing constantly, until tender, about 5 minutes.)

3  While the eggplant cooks, make the sauce by combining the scallion, chile pepper, garlic, soy sauce, sesame seeds, sesame oil and black pepper. Toss the hot eggplant with the sauce and serve.

# Mumallaengi Muchim
## 무말랭이무침

### DRIED DAIKON RADISH MUCHIM

This is a pretty specific radish kimchi that is served primarily with Bossam (crispy pork belly, page 155) and has a distinct texture that is almost like eating a dehydrated mango. It's chewier than a fresh, crisp radish, with a concentrated root-vegetable flavor. It works magic when cutting through the fatty pork. You will notice the near-insane amount of gochugaru required for this recipe. Follow our lead: when mixed with the soy sauce, mirin and aromatics, it merges to create a really nice sauce—with heat and sweetness—that stands up to the mighty powers of the pig. You can find packages of dried daikon radish at most Asian grocery stores. **MAKES 4 CUPS**

1 cup dried daikon radish

1 cup light soy sauce

2 Korean red chile peppers, thinly sliced

½ medium onion, minced

3 Korean green chile peppers, thinly sliced

2 scallions, thinly sliced

6 garlic cloves, minced

1-inch knob of ginger, minced

1 cup coarsely ground gochugaru

½ cup Korean rice or corn syrup

3 tablespoons mirin

3 tablespoons sesame seeds

1  Rehydrate the dried daikon by placing in a large bowl with 5 cups of water and the soy sauce. Allow it to sit covered at room temperature for 30 minutes to 1 hour. It will grow slightly in size and soak up the liquid. Strain, discarding any excess liquid.

2  In a medium bowl, mix together all remaining ingredients until combined. The bright red marinade will be thick and fragrant. Add the rehydrated daikon radish, mixing well. Refrigerate overnight and serve cold. The daikon will keep in the fridge for 2 weeks.

1 tablespoon sesame oil

1 tablespoon coarsely ground gochugaru

1 tablespoon soy sauce

1 tablespoon mirin

2 tablespoons honey

4 garlic cloves, minced

1 tablespoon vegetable oil

½ pound whole shishito peppers, stems removed

½ cup dried anchovies

Sesame seeds, for garnish

# Kkwarigochu Muchim
## 꽈리고추무침

### BLISTERED SHISHITO PEPPERS

This is one of the most addictive banchan dishes around. Shishito peppers are very mild and a bit sweet, but you sometimes can get a really hot one, so there's a little nervous excitement with every bite. We like to make ours with baby anchovies, which offer a hint of brininess that works magic with the honey and soy sauce. Make this, snack on it but leave some for later—the marinated peppers only get better with time. SERVES 4

1 In a small bowl, combine the sesame oil, gochugaru, soy sauce, mirin, honey and half the garlic to make the sauce.

2 Place a large cast-iron pan over high and add the vegetable oil. When the oil is lightly smoking, swirl the oil, add peppers and let them sear until blistered and slightly charred, turning each a few times. Add the dried anchovies and sauce and cook for 30 seconds. Turn off heat and add ¼ cup of water. Stir while the sauce bubbles and garnish with sesame seeds. Allow to cool down to room temperature and serve. This will keep in your refrigerator for up to a week.

¼ cup soy sauce

2 tablespoons sugar

1 tablespoon coarsely ground gochugaru

1 tablespoon Korean rice or corn syrup

2 tablespoons vegetable oil

1 pound fish cakes, cut into thin strips or diamond shapes

2 garlic cloves, minced

1 medium onion, thinly sliced

2 Korean red chile peppers, thinly sliced

2 tablespoons sesame seeds, for garnish

# Eomuk Bokkeum
## 어묵볶음
### SPICY STIR-FRIED FISH CAKE

A popular lunch-box item for Korean children, stir-fried fish cakes often bring back memories of childhood when served as banchan at the dinner table. We like the simplicity of this recipe, as well as the soy-driven sweetness that caramelizes when it hits hot oil. Mmmmm! Fish cakes are sold both fresh and frozen at your local Asian grocery, where you can find a wide variety of shapes. For good or for bad, you can think of them as the hot dog of the sea, made from ground whitefish. For this dish, it's important to buy the thin-cut variety, which is best for stir-frying (thicker ones are used primarily in soups). SERVES 4 TO 6

1 In a small bowl, combine the soy sauce, sugar, gochugaru and rice syrup. This is the sauce.

2 Place a large sauté pan over high heat and add the oil. Once the pan is lightly smoking, add the fish cakes and stir-fry for 2 minutes, tossing frequently until the fish cakes turn a light shade of brown. Add garlic, onion and chile peppers and continue to stir-fry for 3 minutes, until the onions soften. Add the sauce and toss frequently until slightly caramelized, about 2 minutes.

3 Remove from the heat and garnish with sesame seeds. Serve hot or let it cool; it's best served at room temperature. Leftovers will keep up to a week in the fridge.

# Dubu Jorim

## 두부조림

### SOY-BRAISED TOFU

Tofu (called dubu by Koreans) is often praised for its health values. True, eating a lot of tofu—the fresh, GMO-free kind, ideally—will help you live to be 116 years old. But tofu is not just for health nuts (and who really wants to live until they are 116?). It's for fans of cooking with *texture*, and this fried-then-braised tofu dish is just the fix with an incredibly pleasing mouthfeel. After frying the tofu to a pleasant shade of golden brown, we add a highly flavorful sauce that braises and bubbles with the bean curd until it's reached a nice caramelized state. It's a distinctly Korean dish that is best served at room temperature. SERVES 4

1  In a medium bowl, whisk together the soy sauce, garlic, ginger, gochugaru, sesame oil, sugar and mirin.

2  Heat a generous coating of vegetable oil in a large skillet on medium-high heat until lightly smoking. Add tofu, leaving some room between the pieces, and cook until golden brown, turning frequently, for 8 to 10 minutes. Remove the tofu to a paper-towel-lined plate. Repeat with any remaining tofu. Drain all but 1 tablespoon of the oil and add the soy sauce mixture and ½ cup of water. Return the tofu and braise over medium-high heat, until the liquid has reduced to a caramel-like sauce, about 4 minutes. Remove from heat. Serve garnished with scallions and sesame seeds.

1 18-ounce package of firm tofu, cut into ½-inch slices and patted dry with paper towels

¼ cup soy sauce

2 garlic cloves, minced

½-inch knob of ginger, minced

1 tablespoon coarsely ground gochugaru

1 teaspoon sesame oil

2 tablespoons sugar

1 tablespoon mirin

Vegetable oil, as needed

1 teaspoon minced Korean red chile pepper

1 scallion, thinly sliced, for garnish

1 tablespoon sesame seeds, for garnish

# ATLANTA
## BUFORD HIGHWAY FARMERS MARKET

In 1974, Harold Shinn's father opened the first Asian grocery store in Atlanta. The modest shop sold basically everything Asian he could get his hands on: products imported from China, Vietnam, Thailand and especially South Korea, where he immigrated from in the late sixties. In a pre-Amazon era, the shop was a blessing from the food gods for the Asian immigrants who had moved to the cosmopolitan heart of the American South. "When we arrived, there was basically nowhere to shop," recalls Shinn. "My father would make connections by knocking on doors." Fast-forward forty years and the Shinn family is still in the grocery business, though on a scale that echoes Atlanta's swelling Korean American population.

Though the name Buford Highway Farmers Market suggests an open-air assembly of farmers, the 100,000-square-foot building in Doraville—a twenty-minute drive northeast of downtown Atlanta—is like a cross between a gourmet store, Walmart and your favorite Chinatown produce shop. Well, if you also threw in your city's best Polish butcher, Mexican tortilleria, Scandinavian chocolatier and Tokyo's Tsukiji Market. There are discoveries in every aisle, like three types of Russian cola, or a variety of apple grown only in New Zealand. And, of course, the market's Korean section: delicate mandu and soondae made daily in the back, and some of the best banchan in all of Atlanta. "My produce aisle doesn't look like this," said an emphatic Anthony Bourdain while picking through stacks of sesame leaves, watercress and radishes during his pilgrimage.

Harold has been running the market with his family for over two decades and has witnessed the shifting dynamic of Koreans in the Atlanta area, emblematic of the growth of Korean American communities around the country in places like Houston, Seattle and Washington, D.C. According to Shinn, Koreans immigrated to the area for two main reasons. "There are four distinct seasons, but none are quite as extreme as in Korea," he says. But more than the weather, it's been the draw of cheap land and a growing community that drew business-minded Koreans by the tens of thousands. He describes his father as having a "farmer-entrepreneur" spirit, and so he avoided the more-common and more-crowded Los Angeles, New York City or Chicago immigration path. He recounts how, in the booming 1970s, groups of guys who went to the same college in Korea would move together and open up adjacent businesses. "And if you were not part of this class, there was a sense that you did not make it."

Eventually, the Korean population that had settled along Buford Highway hit a critical mass, sending both established families and new immigrants up the road to Duluth, now home to one of the fastest-growing Koreatowns in America. According to the 2010 Census, between 2000 and 2010 the Korean population in Georgia grew 86 percent; Korean is the third most-spoken language in the state, after English and Spanish. A massive change from a time, as Shinn describes it, that "there would be weeks between seeing another Korean family."

4 eggs

1 teaspoon kosher salt

¾ cup Anchovy Stock
(page 195)

1 tablespoon thinly sliced
scallions

# Gyeran Jjim
## 계란찜
### BUBBLING EGG

Gyeran jjim is a popular banchan that arrives with great ceremony to begin a meal, a bubbling-hot crock of savory custard, definitively eggy, but with a faint reminder of the sea. The texture is somewhere between poached and scrambled, and it is often the first solid food a Korean mother will feed her newborn child. But for the adults sitting around a crowded Koreatown barbecue joint, it's the banchan everybody wants more of, but is afraid to ask for. Some servers will frown at the request or may even shoot you a dirty look. But that's the beauty of making this simple dish at home: if you run out, just crack a few eggs and enjoy round two. **SERVES 4**

**1** In a small bowl, beat together the eggs and salt.

**2** In a small pot or saucepan, bring the stock to a rolling boil over medium heat. Pour in the egg mixture, stirring constantly until small curds start to form and the mixture resembles watery scrambled eggs. Stop stirring and immediately reduce the heat to low. Cover the pot and cook for 1 minute. Remove from heat, but keep it covered and take it to the table. The egg should be moist but firm and bubbling.

**3** Stir in the scallions and serve immediately.

# Gamja Saelleodeu

## 감자샐러드

### POTATO SALAD

Potato salad has been a banchan favorite at Korean restaurants in America for generations, not only because it's affordable to make—a necessity for bottom-line-driven owners—but also because it's such a unique, mellow contrast to all the in-your-face kimchis, pickles and fermented fish. When we're eating out in Koreatown with friends, it's often the first plate to be emptied. Our recipe marries the sweetness and freshness of apples and carrots with the richness of mayonnaise and egg. And here's a little secret from Deuki's mom: a little bit of Korean yogurt drink (sold under the brand name Biofeel or Yakult) adds sweetness and a flavor that is definitively Korean. If you can't find it, don't stress. But if you can, it's pretty much the best in potato salad to go along with your Korean feast. **SERVES 4**

**1** Bring a small pot of water to a boil. Add eggs and boil for 12 minutes. Run them under cold water to cool, and peel them. Separate the whites and yolks and small dice the whites. Crumble the egg yolks and reserve them for garnish.

**2** Bring a large pot of lightly salted water to a boil. Boil potatoes for 15 to 20 minutes, or until tender and a fork can be inserted easily and comes out clean.

**3** While still warm, mash the potatoes with a fork, leaving a few larger chunks for texture. Place the potatoes in a bowl and mix in the sugar, salt and pepper. Set aside to cool.

**4** Core and cut the apple into small dice. To the bowl with the smashed potatoes add the egg whites, corn, carrot, mayonnaise and yogurt drink and mix well. Add more salt and pepper to taste. Garnish with crumbled egg yolks.

2 eggs

2 medium russet potatoes, peeled and halved

1 teaspoon sugar

2 teaspoons kosher salt, plus more to taste

½ teaspoon black pepper, plus more to taste

1 apple (Fuji or Gala preferred)

½ cup drained canned corn

1 medium carrot, cut into small dice

¾ cup good mayonnaise like Hellmann's or Best Foods

2 tablespoons Biofeel or Yakult yogurt drink (optional)

8 blue crabs

2 tablespoons soju

3 tablespoons kosher salt

8 dried Korean red chile peppers, stems removed

1 small onion, thinly sliced

½ Asian pear, cored and roughly chopped

5 garlic cloves

1-inch knob of ginger, roughly chopped

¼ cup finely ground gochugaru

1 tablespoon mirin

1 tablespoon sesame seeds

1 tablespoon sugar

¼ cup Korean rice or corn syrup

½ tablespoon black pepper

2 scallions, trimmed and sliced into 2-inch batons

# Yangnyeom Gejang
## 양념 게장
### SPICY MARINATED CRABS

Allow us to introduce you to one of the supreme Korean seafood traditions: raw crabs. In Seoul there are specific streets lined with restaurants specializing in ganjang gejang ("crabs marinated in soy sauce") and its spicier cousin, yangnyeom gejang, which we have here. It is quite an experience to crack into a marinated blue crab for the first time—sucking out the raw meat and bright orange roe. While Americans are more accustomed to boiled or steamed crab, the raw, ceviche-like preparation is remarkably sweeter, while the sauce contrasts nicely with slap-you-in-the-face spice. The crab, in all its messy glory, is always served with rice, which is packed into the bodies and mixed together with the last bits of meat and roe. Guys, it's so good.

Making yangnyeom gejang at home is relatively straightforward but requires some advance planning. First, it's essential to find the freshest crabs available, ideally still alive—which you can find at good seafood stores and Asian supermarkets. In America, the blue crab season runs from spring until early fall, but you can likely find them year-round. If possible, you want to use only mature female crabs (packed with delicious roe), which can be identified by a dome-like pattern on their abdomen. Once the crabs have arrived in your kitchen, place them in the freezer for at least an hour. This will slow them down and make them easier to handle. Then it's time to clean the crabs (see below). From there, it's a simple 1 to 2 days in the marinade until the crabs are ready for you to crack into them. Either pick out the tender meat with chopsticks or go full native and suck it out. And don't forget the rice!
SERVES 4

l  Freeze the crabs for 1 to 2 hours, but no longer. Under continuously running cold water, scrub the crabs thoroughly with a toothbrush and rinse several times. Using heavy kitchen shears, cut off the eyes. Cut off the tips of the legs but not the entire leg. Flip the crab onto its back and remove the apron, which looks like a tail flattened into the body, and clean out the gills and entrails. The gills are the frilly things you see when you open the crabs. Cut the crabs in half.

**2** Place the crabs in a large bowl with the soju and 2 tablespoons of the salt. Refrigerate for 10 minutes.

**3** While the crabs cure, make the marinade by pureeing the chile peppers, onion, Asian pear, garlic and ginger. Place in a bowl. Add the gochugaru, mirin, sesame seeds, sugar, syrup, black pepper and remaining tablespoon of salt.

**4** Rinse crabs of the soju-salt cure. In a large resealable container, combine the marinade with the blue crabs and scallions. Place in the refrigerator for 1 to 2 days; the marinade will turn a darker shade of red. Now it is time to get messy with it.

1 cup Korean pancake mix

1 cup ice-cold sparkling water

1 cup diced extra-aged kimchi

½ cup kimchi juice

1 egg yolk

1 tablespoon doenjang

1 teaspoon coarsely ground gochugaru

1 medium onion, thinly sliced

Vegetable oil, as needed

Jeon Dipping Sauce (recipe follows), for serving

# Kimchi Jeon

## 김치전

### KIMCHI PANCAKE

Crisp and chewy pancakes are an incredibly popular menu item at Korean restaurants. They are fun to pull apart and offer diners little hints of kimchi (or scallions and seafood), mellowed out with crunch and elevated by a soy-vinegar sauce. Note: You sometimes have to ask for the sauce if the busy servers forget. Never let this happen.

But. Most pancakes you find in American restaurants, and we're talking about 70 to 80 percent here, are (1) usually burnt and (2) way too doughy! Let us show you how to make them right. We're starting with the most basic, kimchi jeon. By using extra-fermented kimchi and a nice amount of kimchi juice, the pancake really packs a lot of flavor.

We use packaged pancake mix, which is available at any Korean grocery. We like how the mix of flour, baking powder, cornstarch and light seasoning binds together and tastes . . . and in our experience, almost all Korean restaurants and homes use it too, so this will give you the flavor you know and love. The real key is finding the right ratio of vegetables or seafood to dough. We aim for just enough batter to bring the filling together. When frying, it's important to follow our method: take refrigerated batter and drop into a hot pan *before* lowering the heat. This will help to cook the pancake evenly, with crisping throughout. And always keep your eye on the prize at all times, as they can burn quite quickly if the flame gets out of control. **MAKES 8 SMALL PANCAKES**

1 In a large bowl, combine all ingredients except for the oil and dipping sauce and refrigerate for 15 minutes to allow everything to mingle and marry. Preheat the oven to warm, or the lowest temperature setting.

2 Generously slick a large cast-iron skillet with vegetable oil and heat it over medium-high heat. When the oil shimmers, drop ½ cup of batter into the pan for each pancake. Drop the heat to medium-low and fry 4 to 5 minutes until light golden brown along the edges, then flip and fry the other side for another 3 to 4 minutes, until also golden and the pancake is cooked through. Fry longer if you like it crispier, but take care not to let it get too dark. Repeat with remaining batter, stirring between additions, and reheating and oiling the pan between batches.

**3** Remove pancakes from the skillet and place on a paper-towel-lined plate, turning them once to remove the excess oil. Place the pancake on a cutting board and cut to your preferred size and shape (we like ours squared off). Keep pancakes warm in the oven while you make the rest. Serve with Jeon Dipping Sauce.

## JEON DIPPING SAUCE

**3 tablespoons rice vinegar**

**3 tablespoons soy sauce**

**3 teaspoons sesame oil**

**2 teaspoons finely ground gochugaru**

**2 teaspoons toasted sesame seeds**

Combine all ingredients in a small bowl. This will keep in the fridge indefinitely. MAKES ABOUT ½ CUP

1 cup Korean pancake mix

1 cup ice-cold sparkling water

1 egg yolk

1 tablespoon doenjang

Vegetable oil, as needed

1 bunch scallions, trimmed and cut into 2-inch batons

Kosher salt to taste

Jeon Dipping Sauce (page 67), for serving

# Pajeon
## 파전
### SCALLION PANCAKE

The pajeon, milder than Kimchi Jeon (page 66), is also a favorite at Korean restaurants. Unlike the kimchi version, where a single batter is poured onto a hot griddle, we think of this as a two-part process: char the scallion, then add the batter. This will give each pancake a set of nicely browned scallions (which is pretty much the best way to eat scallions, are we right?) without burning the outside. It also looks pretty cool when you line them up in a crisscross pattern. MAKES 4 MEDIUM PANCAKES

1 In a medium bowl, combine pancake mix, sparkling water, egg yolk and doenjang. Refrigerate for 15 minutes. Preheat the oven to warm, or the lowest temperature setting.

2 In a small frying pan, heat 1 tablespoon of oil over medium-high heat. Add scallions in one layer and cook, flipping once, until charred. (Work in batches if necessary.) Season scallions with salt and set aside.

3 Generously slick a large cast-iron skillet with vegetable oil and heat over medium-high heat. When the oil shimmers, drop ½ cup of batter into the pan for each pancake. Line charred scallions in the batter in a handsome pattern.

4 Drop the heat to medium-low and fry 4 to 5 minutes, until light golden brown along the edges, then flip and fry the other side for another 3 to 4 minutes, until golden and the pancake is cooked through. Fry longer if you like it crispier, but take care not to let it get too dark. Repeat with remaining batter, stirring between additions, and reheating and oiling the pan between batches.

5 Remove pancakes from the oil and place on a paper-towel-lined plate, turning once to remove excess oil. Place the pancake on a cutting board and cut to your preferred size and shape (we like ours squared off). Keep finished pancakes warm in the oven while you cook the rest. Serve with a small bowl of Jeon Dipping Sauce.

# Haemul Pajeon
## 해물파전
### SEAFOOD PANCAKE

This variation of the pajeon introduces squid and baby shrimp to the party. Instead of water, we like to use Anchovy Stock for an extra burst of ocean brine (although sparkling water will work as well). Haemul pajeon pairs particularly well with soju. How do we know? A wise ajumma once told us, and we are not going to debate her. **MAKES 6 TO 8 SMALL PANCAKES**

1   In a medium bowl, combine pancake mix, stock, egg yolk, doenjang, squid, shrimp and scallions. Refrigerate for 15 minutes. Preheat oven to warm, or the lowest temperature setting.

2   Generously slick a large heavy skillet with vegetable oil and heat over medium-high heat. When the oil shimmers, drop ½ cup of batter into the pan for each pancake. Drop the heat to medium-low and fry 4 to 5 minutes, until light golden brown along the edges, then flip and fry the other side for another 3 to 4 minutes, until golden brown and the pancake and seafood are cooked through. Fry longer if you like it crispier, but take care not to let it get too dark. Repeat with remaining batter, stirring between additions, and reheating and oiling the pan between batches.

3   Remove pancakes from the oil and place on a paper-towel-lined plate, turning once to remove excess oil. Place the pancake on a cutting board and cut to your preferred size and shape (we like ours squared off). Keep finished pancakes warm in the oven while you cook the rest. Serve with Jeon Dipping Sauce.

**1 cup Korean pancake mix**

**1 cup cooled Anchovy Stock (page 000) or ice-cold sparkling water**

**1 egg yolk**

**1 tablespoon doenjang**

**½ pound squid, cut into 2-inch pieces**

**¼ pound baby shrimp**

**1 bunch scallions, trimmed and cut into 2-inch batons**

**Vegetable oil, as needed**

**Jeon Dipping Sauce (page 67), for serving**

# Rice, Noodles & Dumplings

밥, 국수 & 만두

**K**oreatown Plaza, a shopping center with a plain facade that hides its inner curiosities, is located on a busy corner of Western Avenue and San Marino Street in the heart of Los Angeles's Koreatown. Around eighty stores fill up its three floors, including small streetwear boutiques, a United Colors of Benetton and several family-owned shops and kiosks catering specifically to the city's vibrant Korean population—there's a music store hawking Girls' Generation CDs and Super Junior posters to packs of K-pop-loving teenagers.

But it's in the windowless basement where the serious action is going down. Mall food courts, in general, are pretty depressing affairs—down to the permanent smell of Cinnabon. But in some Korean American communities, food courts serve an important function as a place to grab a quick bite to eat, but also to play some cards, watch a teledrama on community TV screens and socialize over steaming bowls of noodles and dumplings.

At the food court at Koreatown Plaza, Pao Jao Dumpling House is one of the most popular stalls, built on the reputation of their superior black bean noodles called jjajangmyeon and giant dumplings called king mandu, stuffed with pork, glass noodles, scallions and *a lot* of garlic. When the pouches of dough are torn into, fragrant steam perfumes the surrounding tables.

Both mandu and jjajangmyeon are examples of how Korean cooking extends well beyond grilled meat. Koreans have an undying passion for noodles and dumplings that rivals their neighbors in China and Japan. In this chapter we include our own recipe for doctoring up Shin Ramyun (Korea's most-popular instant brand). There are literally a thousand ways to make it.

But as much as Koreans love their ramyun, it all begins with rice. Because many, many Koreans don't consider a meal to be a *meal* if there isn't rice involved. So, in this chapter we've got cast-iron toasted rice cakes, a crazy delicious kimchi and bacon fried rice and raw fish served over rice with a homemade sauce, chojang. And, of course, there's bibimbap. 틉

# Bap
## 밥
RICE

2 cups medium- or short-grain rice

2½ cups water

A visit to the rice aisle of any Asian grocery store will present you with many choices. There is country of origin: South Korea, China, Japan, Thailand, Sri Lanka, India, Texas. There is grain size: short, medium, long. Then there are the varieties, with some 30,000 in existence. Rose-matta versus dinorado anyone? Rice is critical in the Korean kitchen, which is why we want to show you how to cook rice on the stovetop. Of course there are great electric rice cookers available, and most Koreans use them, but not everyone's made the investment.

A couple things to keep in mind: Koreans use a short or medium grain. (The shorter the grain, the stickier the rice.) And before you cook rice, you must properly rinse it. This is something that many Western home cooks forget, but it's crucial in removing extra starches, which is the first step in avoiding gluey rice. **SERVES 4**

1 Place the rice in a large bowl and run plenty of cold water over it, moving your hands through the grains like you're scratching the head of a kitten. The liquid will turn cloudy. Tilt the bowl and discard the first batch of rice water down the drain. Repeat two or three times until the water runs clear, reserving these passes of rice water, if you'd like, for thickening soups and stews. Drain the rice.

2 Add the washed rice to a wide pot or stone bowl (suitable for cooking) and add 2½ cups water. As an aside, Koreans have a long tradition of cooking without measurements called son-mat (translation: "the taste of one's hands"). To measure water this way, place your hand on top of the rice and allow the water to fill until it covers the spot where your fingers and hand meet, just at the start of your knuckle.

3 Allow the rice and water to sit for 30 minutes, which lets the rice absorb some of the water and return to room temperature.

4 Over high heat, bring the pot of rice to a full boil, then drop to a simmer over very low heat (an occasional bubble is OK). Cover and cook for 10 minutes. Take the pot completely off the heat and allow it to sit, covered, for 10 minutes before serving. The cooked rice should be sticky, but you should be able to discern the individual grains.

½ pound of slab bacon, roughly chopped

1 medium onion, cut into small dice

2 garlic cloves, minced

1-inch knob of ginger, minced

1½ cups chopped extra-aged Napa Cabbage Kimchi (page 41)

2 cups cooked rice, preferably day-old

1 tablespoon gochujang

2 tablespoons butter, softened

2 eggs, fried sunny-side up

2 scallions, sliced thin

# Our Mildly Insane Kimchi Bokkeumbap
## 김치볶음밥
### KIMCHI FRIED RICE

Bacon. We kept coming back to bacon when talking about this kimchi fried-rice recipe. Bacon is quintessential Americana. Our kimchi fried rice *needed* bacon, and for months we tested and were continually disappointed that the essence of bacon—Americana!—was being muted by either too much rice or too much kimchi. Then it came to us. We needed to use more bacon! Like a lot more. Like how French chefs view mashed potatoes: equal parts butter and potatoes. That's scary, right? Also scary good.

We went that direction here and by the grace of god and Allan Benton did this ever work. The crispy rice unites with the decadent gochujang butter, while the bacon is there just being wonderful. And remember, the key to good fried rice is using cold day-old rice, which is nice and dried out and gives you a much better fry. So the next time you order takeout, get an extra order of rice and keep it in the fridge for a day or so. And if you didn't plan ahead, no sweat. Make some rice and lay it out on a sheet tray and freeze until cold. SERVES 2

1  In a large skillet, wok or cast-iron pan over high heat, cook the bacon, stirring, until fat is fully rendered and the bacon is barely starting to crisp. Pour out all but 2 tablespoons fat.

2  Add onion, garlic and ginger and sauté for 1 minute, or until very aromatic. Add chopped kimchi and rice and sauté, stirring frequently, for 4 to 5 minutes, or until very hot. Drop the heat to medium-low and flatten the rice with your spatula. Continue to cook until the bottom layer is crispy, about 2 minutes; think Spanish paella here. The longer you leave it, the more crispy the bottom will become, but be careful not to burn the garlic.

3  While the rice continues to crisp, in a small bowl mix together the gochujang and softened butter.

4  Serve from the pan or wok, topped with fried eggs, sliced scallions and gochujang butter.

# Yachae Juk

## 야채죽

VEGETABLE RICE PORRIDGE

Juk is a fortifying porridge, like Chinese congee in texture, that plays counter to many common principles in Korean cooking. First off, there are no strong fermented jangs involved. Spice is completely absent. Instead, juk is a more restorative dish—the food mom makes for you when you're sick—and a comforting union of rice and vegetables. Simple to make and eat and gone before you know it. Juk is made with many different components, including pumpkin, red bean and, at its most rarefied, abalone. Our version is basic: vegetables, dried seaweed, soy sauce for seasoning. We like using white beech (Bunapi) mushrooms, but you can substitute any mushrooms, such as chopped shiitake, enoki or cremini. SERVES 4

1 Soak the rice in cold water to cover for 1 hour, then drain well.

2 In a heavy medium saucepan, heat 1 tablespoon of sesame oil over high heat until it is lightly smoking. Add the garlic, ginger and mushrooms and sauté for 30 seconds, until fragrant. Add the carrots, onions and zucchini and saute for 3 minutes, or until onions are translucent. Season with salt and pepper.

3 Add the drained rice and the remaining sesame oil and toast slightly, stirring, for another minute.

4 Add the stock and bring to a boil. Drop the heat to a simmer and cook, stirring occasionally, until the liquid has reduced and the rice is tender and has taken on a porridge-like consistency, about 15 minutes. Season to taste with salt and pepper.

5 Divide juk into bowls and garnish with toasted seaweed and sesame seeds. Serve with soy sauce on the side.

1 cup short-grain rice

2 tablespoons sesame oil

2 garlic cloves, minced

1-inch knob of ginger, grated

½ cup whole Bunapi mushrooms

½ cup small-diced carrots

½ cup small-diced onions

½ cup small-diced zucchini

Kosher salt and black pepper to taste

6 cups vegetable stock or Anchovy Stock (page 195)

1 large sheet toasted nori or gim, cut into thin strips

1 teaspoon toasted sesame seeds

Soy sauce, for serving

½ cup gochujang

2 teaspoons sesame oil

1 tablespoon honey

1 tablespoon sugar

1 tablespoon Korean apple vinegar or rice vinegar

1 tablespoon lemon-lime soda

FOR THE RICE AND SUGGESTED TOPPINGS

2 cups hot cooked rice

½ carrot, julienned

½ cup Soy and Sesame Spinach (page 48), room temperature

½ cup Crunchy Sesame Bean Sprouts (page 51), room temperature

½ cup Napa Cabbage Kimchi (page 41), room temperature

1 cup Bulgogi (page 118), warm or room temperature

2 or 3 fried eggs

2 or 3 small sheets of toasted seaweed, cut into thin strips

Sesame seeds to taste

# This Is Not a Bibimbap Recipe
## 비빔밥
### MIXED RICE BOWL

Outside of barbecue and kimchi, bibimbap is quite possibly the best-known Korean dish in America—with versions being served from Asian-fusion restaurants to Applebee's. And what's not to love? Mixing warm rice with a bunch of pickled, seasoned and fresh vegetables, grilled meat and a fried egg simply blankets your soul. But here's the thing about bibimbap (or Triple B as we like to call it): there really isn't a definitive recipe. The name translates to "mixed rice," and, in practice, rice is the dish's only constant. What else can you put on top of the rice? That extra portion of bulgogi or sautéed squid—perfect, there's your meat. Seasoned bean sprouts, cucumber kimchi, that half package of fish cakes you found in the back of your freezer. Good, good, good. Got a package of seasoned dried seaweed from Trader Joe's? Crumble it up for a topping. And, of course, there's the special sauce.

When Deuki was growing up, his mom would make bibimbap as a way to clean out the fridge at the end of a long week of cooking. When Deuki moved out of the house, working long hours at Momofuku Noodle Bar and Jean-Georges, he'd prepare a version upon returning home early in the morning. This is more an "anti-recipe" because it just serves as a basic guideline. You can make it as simple, or complicated, as you would like. We've also included a recipe for a sweet-and-spicy sauce that gives the dish its trademark shade and, in some cases, heat. You can adjust that to your liking. **SERVES 2 TO 3**

1  **MAKE THE SAUCE:** Whisk together the gochujang, sesame oil, honey, sugar, vinegar and lemon-lime soda. Set aside.

2  **BUILD YOUR BOWLS:** Divide the rice into bowls and top with the vegetables, Bulgogi, fried eggs, toasted seaweed, sesame seeds and sauce to taste (some like more than others, but start with 2 tablespoons for each serving, enough to just turn the rice a light red when mixed in).

3  Mix well with a spoon, integrating the vegetable, meat, sauce and egg into a gooey, crunchy, amazing ball of goodness.

½ small white onion

1 large carrot

1 cucumber, peeled

1 head red leaf or
romaine lettuce

6 perilla leaves

8 4 × 4-inch squares
dried nori seaweed

½ pound sushi-grade
salmon

½ pound sushi-grade
tuna

2 cups cooked short-
grain rice, warm

½ cup masago or tobiko
(fish roe)

2 teaspoons sesame
seeds

½ cup Chojang (recipe
follows)

1 lemon, quartered

# Hoedeopbap
## 회덮밥
### SASHIMI RICE BOWL

South Korea is a country with a vast coastline, some 3,000 miles in total. So while barbecue beef and blistering soups are most commonly associated with the peninsula's cuisine, seafood plays an even more important role and Koreans covet the freshest seafood possible. So fresh that there's a long tradition of Korean fish-tank restaurants that specialize in saengseon hoe, which is essentially the Korean version of sashimi. Diners give their order, and the chefs pull out the fish, butcher it and serve. Unlike the raw fish served in Japanese style, where it is aged from days to weeks, saengseon hoe is a bit tougher; as with all freshly killed meat, rigor mortis soon sets in, which adds toughness to the flesh. For Koreans, the chewiness is all part of the deal. But because you won't likely be killing your dinner moments before serving it, we've compromised with one of our favorite raw fish dishes that you can easily make at home.

Hoedeopbap is like the raw-fish version of bibimbap. Start with the best raw fish you can find, typically described as sushi grade. We like salmon and tuna, but you can seek out whatever you like. (Remember, when buying fish, if you smell anything that resembles "fishy" at all, avoid it; the fish should smell clean and sweet.) Briny fish roe and crisp vegetables add layers of complexity, and tying everything together is homemade chojang, a sweet and spicy condiment that is sold in a red squeeze bottle at all Korean grocery stores and is a fixture at tank restaurants. While the bottled version is fine if you are in a pinch, we suggest making our version, which combines the satisfying sweetness of pineapple juice with gochujang and rice vinegar, which cuts beautifully through the fatty salmon and tuna. **SERVES 4**

1  Slice the onion paper thin on a mandoline and julienne the carrot. Soak them in ice water so they remain fresh and crisp. Slice the cucumber into half-moons and roughly chop the lettuce and perilla leaves. Using scissors, shear the dried seaweed into thin strips. Set all aside.

2 Using a very sharp knife, slice salmon and tuna into ¼-inch slices and place on a chilled plate.

3 Divide the warm (not steaming-hot) rice into 4 bowls. Add lettuce, perilla leaves and cucumber. Remove onions and carrots from the ice bath and shake them dry before adding them to the bowls. Place the raw fish and masago in the center and garnish with dried seaweed and sesame seeds. Drizzle some Chojang in each bowl. (You will have some left that you might want to add later.) Mix everything together and serve with lemon wedges.

**¼ cup gochujang**

**¼ cup rice vinegar**

**2 tablespoons sugar**

**2 tablespoons pineapple juice (substituting orange juice is OK)**

## CHOJANG (VINEGAR GOCHUJANG SAUCE)

Chojang is a sweet-and-spicy condiment served alongside a number of classic Korean dishes like bibimbap and hoedeopbap. It's also great for punching up a snoozy plate of steamed vegetables, or as a dipping sauce for grilled meat. New York City chef Hooni Kim (of Danji and Hanjan) smartly calls it the "mother of all seafood sauces" and uses it in many dishes at his groundbreaking Manhattan restaurants. While you can buy chojang in the bottle, our homemade version combines the distinct sweetness of pineapple juice with rice vinegar and gochujang, which is available in many different levels of spice; we suggest using mild for this recipe. **MAKES ABOUT ½ CUP**

Combine gochujang, vinegar, sugar and pineapple juice in a bowl and whisk together until fully combined. The texture should be smooth with no chunks of gochujang remaining. Leftover sauce keeps for up to 1 week, refrigerated.

# Cast-Iron Ddeokbokki
## 떡볶이
### TOASTED RICE CAKES

These plump and chewy rice cakes bear a resemblance to Italian gnocchi. Typically they are sautéed and served in a spicy, fragrant sauce consisting mostly of gochujang and sugar. Over the years we've also spotted a number of unorthodox preparations: deep-fried on a skewer, cooked with soy-based sauce and, a favorite of ours, topped with a couple fistfuls of awesomely industrial mozzarella cheese and strips of seared pork—as found at one of our favorite New York City Koreatown restaurants, Arang. Korean nachos!

In South Korea rice cakes are a popular snack sold at street stands and pojangmachas, the ubiquitous tent restaurants stationed along the streets that sell late into the night. In Koreatown, the dish heads indoors but is equally popular with the drunk and insatiable.

Our recipe is inspired by the ddeokbokki served at Seoul's Tongin Market: finished in an extremely hot wok for extra crispiness and glazed with a sweet-spicy-savory sauce. Buy the frozen thick, dowel-like ddeokbokki for this dish; the dried ones are used in soups. SERVES 4

1 In a medium bowl, whisk together the stock, gochujang, syrup, gochugaru, soy sauce, mirin, honey powder and garlic.

2 Soak the frozen rice cakes in water overnight. If you are in a pinch, bring a pot of water to a boil and boil the cakes for 8 to 10 minutes. After boiling, the rice cakes must be used immediately.

3 Dry the rice cakes very well on paper towels. In a wok or large cast-iron pan over high heat, heat the vegetable oil until it is lightly smoking. Add the rice cakes and let them sear until light golden brown, then toss and let sear again until the other side is lightly crisped, about 3 minutes on each side. Add the fish cakes and cook for another 2 minutes, until heated through. Add the cabbage, onions and carrots and cook until softened, about 3 minutes.

4 Pour the reserved sauce over the mixture and simmer over medium-high heat until the sauce has thickened, about 2 minutes. Serve with the eggs, scallions and sesame seeds.

FOR THE SAUCE

**½ cup Anchovy Stock (page 195)**

**3 tablespoons gochujang**

**3 tablespoons Korean rice or corn syrup**

**1 tablespoon coarsely ground gochugaru**

**1 tablespoon soy sauce**

**1 tablespoon mirin**

**1 tablespoon honey powder or sugar**

**2 garlic cloves, minced**

FOR THE RICE CAKES

**2 cups frozen rice cakes**

**2 tablespoons vegetable oil**

**¾ cup fish cakes cut into 1-inch pieces**

**½ cup thinly sliced green cabbage**

**½ cup thinly sliced onions**

**¼ cup thinly sliced carrots**

**2 eggs, soft-boiled and halved**

**2 scallions, thinly sliced**

**½ tablespoon toasted sesame seeds**

½ pound dried sweet potato noodles

Kosher salt to taste

½ pound fresh spinach

2 cups plus 3 tablespoons vegetable oil

1 cup thinly sliced fresh shiitake mushrooms

2 garlic cloves, minced

½ cup chopped onions

½ cup julienned carrots

1 cup shredded oyster mushrooms

1 cup trimmed white beech (Bunapi) mushrooms, trimmed and separated

½ cup enoki mushrooms

3 tablespoons mirin

3 tablespoons oyster sauce

3 tablespoons soy sauce, plus more for serving

1 scallion, thinly sliced

1 teaspoon sesame oil

Sesame seeds to taste

# Japchae
## 버섯잡채
### WOK-FRIED GLASS NOODLES WITH CRISPY SHIITAKES

OMG, Asian noodles. Ramen, dan dan, bánh canh, laksa! Regretfully, nobody thinks of japchae with so much excitement, which is really a shame because it's one of our favorite Korean dishes—period. This collective shrug is likely because it is often featured as a banchan at restaurants and frequently overlooked as the main event. This should not be the case, because japchae is absolutely delicious. It's mild, chewy and slightly sweet, similar to the Americanized version of pad Thai we know you love. It's also simple to make. There is no long-simmering broth involved or exotic herbs to procure. Per tradition, large platters are oftentimes brought to parties and celebrations like christenings, birthday parties and backyard barbecues. We think it's time to put this dish on the pedestal it deserves.

The dish is built around sweet potato noodles called dangmyeon, which are gluten-free (success!) and can be found easily at Asian grocery stores. While japchae is often served with bulgogi, we're keeping our vegetarian friends happy and using a medley of earthy mushrooms, including crispy shiitakes, for great texture. The fried shiitakes add a really nice textural element, but if you are short on time, you can skip that step (it's worth it though, promise). SERVES 4

1  In a stockpot, bring a gallon of water to a boil over high heat. Add the noodles and boil about 6 minutes, until tender but chewy. Using tongs or a strainer, remove noodles but keep the water boiling, and run the noodles under cold water until cool; drain well. Add enough salt to the boiling water to make it pleasantly salty. Fill a bowl with ice water and set it nearby. Blanch the spinach for 30 seconds, or until tender and bright green. Remove and shock in the ice water. Drain, squeeze dry and set aside.

2  Heat 2 cups vegetable oil over high heat in a heavy medium saucepan with a few inches of clearance. When the oil reaches 350°F on a frying thermometer, fry the shiitake mushrooms in batches until they turn golden brown and crisp, 1 to 2 minutes. Remove the mushrooms with

a slotted spoon, drain on a paper-towel-lined plate and season them well with salt.

3 In a large sauté or cast-iron pan, heat 2 tablespoons of vegetable oil over high heat. When shimmering-hot, add the garlic and sauté, stirring until fragrant. Add onion and carrots and sauté for 2 minutes, stirring frequently until slightly softened. Add oyster, Bunapi and enoki mushrooms and sauté for 2 minutes, until softened. Add cooked noodles and sauté, stirring, for 2 minutes, then let cook undisturbed for 1 to 2 minutes so the noodles color slightly. Continue cooking—the level of browning is a matter of personal preference.

4 Add the blanched spinach and mirin, oyster sauce and soy sauce, dropping the heat to medium and tossing everything to combine, about 1 minute. Remove from the heat and stir in the scallion, sesame oil and sesame seeds and top with the fried shiitake mushrooms. Season with additional soy sauce to taste.

# Kongguksu
## 콩국수
### SOY MILK NOODLE SOUP

1 cup dried soybeans

2 tablespoons pine nuts

¼ cup sugar

2 tablespoons kosher salt

4 cups water

2 bundles somen noodles

½ cucumber, peeled and julienned

½ carrot, julienned

1 red apple, cored and thinly sliced

2 eggs, hard-boiled

1 tablespoon sesame seeds

We know it might be a little difficult to get totally excited about Soy Milk Noodle Soup. It doesn't really roll off the tongue like cookie-dough ice cream or seven-layer nacho dip. But you have to trust us here: there is nothing more refreshing and fortifying than a bowl done right, somehow rich and light at the same time. Kongguksu is a cold soup traditionally served in the summertime and made with soy milk, thin somen wheat noodles and pine nuts. It's similar to a Japanese chilled soba: light, restrained, healthier than richer broths but very satisfying in its own way. Koreans believe that the chilled soy milk is helpful in restoring energy during the blistering summer heat, so slurp up to power up. **SERVES 4**

1 Soak the soybeans in 6 cups of water for 6 hours to overnight at room temperature. Drain.

2 In a medium saucepan, cover the soaked soybeans with water, bring to a boil over high heat and boil for 20 minutes.

3 While the soybeans boil, toast the pine nuts in a small, dry sauté pan over medium heat, shaking the pan. When the nuts turn a dark shade of brown (but not burnt!) and smell like toasted-nut wonderfulness, remove from the pan and set aside.

4 Drain the boiled soybeans and shock them in a bowl of cold water. Drain the beans and then rub them together with your hands to loosen the skins; remove and discard the skins.

5 In a blender or food processor, puree the boiled soybeans with the pine nuts, sugar and salt. Add 4 cups of water and blend until smooth. (Divide and work in batches if this amount doesn't fit in your blender.) Refrigerate until completely chilled, about 2 hours.

6 While the soybean mixture chills, bring a large pot of water to a boil over high heat and add the somen noodles. Boil for 2 minutes, or as instructed on the packaging. Drain and shock in cold water. Drain again and reserve.

7 Divide the noodles and the soybean broth among bowls. Serve with cucumber, carrots, apples, half a hard-boiled egg and sesame seeds.

# Q&A
## DONT TELL DAVID CHANG HE'S A KOREAN CHEF

There is not a single chef in America more associated with Korean food than David Chang of Momofuku. He has won every major award presented to chefs and runs insanely successful restaurants in New York City, Toronto and Sydney, all known for riffing on iconic Korean ingredients and dishes like rice cakes, gochujang and ssams from pork to porgy. But if you ask Chang, a proud Korean American born outside Washington, D.C., he is absolutely not, by any means, a Korean chef. As Chang tells Matt, his relationship with Korean food and culture is "complicated."

**When Korean food was made in your household as a child, was it a big event?**

Food was just something that I never thought about. It was always just good. The only times I would really notice was when there was some type of holiday or a birthday. My grandma would always try to help my mom make mandu, or when my mom used to make kimchi, all of her friends and aunts would come in to make it. So that was pretty cool. But it was just like, that's what we do. We didn't make that much American food, and if we made anything else, we made Japanese food. That was from my grandfather, who didn't like Korean food.

**Really, why?**

I was raised mostly by my grandparents, and my grandfather was a government official who came from a really well-reared family, and such as it was at the time, the Japanese basically brainwashed him, took him to Japan and taught him everything Japanese when he was a kid. So he never grew up eating Korean food. He actually was taught to dislike it intensely. That's how I grew up eating. My first love has always been Japanese food.

I've been writing this book for a couple of years, and people always ask me: "Is Momofuku the best Korean restaurant in America?" And I'm always like, Momofuku is not a Korean restaurant. And people are confused. You obviously have Korean elements, but your background with Japanese food and your love of Japanese food contradicts that a bit. Because they are so different.

Yeah, that's one part, but another thing is I never wanted to be thought of as a Korean chef. It's like being typecast as a *Star Trek* character—you'll never do anything else for the rest of your life. It's the same if you just do Italian food, you're sort of one-dimensional. Even though I like Korean food and it certainly inspired a lot of the stuff I did early on, I didn't respect it as much. That's really foolish to say now, but at the time I wanted to stay as far away from it as possible.

**Well, ten years ago when you opened Momofuku Noodle Bar, it was a different landscape. Korean restaurants, especially in New York, weren't that great. Disagree with me if you want, but . . .**

No, they're still not good! And sometimes I have thoughts of opening like a really fucking intimate, real Korean restaurant. You know. There would be no reinterpretation of anything. But, I would get bored.

**You would get bored because it wouldn't offer you a little bit of crossover, you wouldn't have the Southern products that you love so much. Japan wouldn't enter the picture . . .**

The problem is that I want to avoid dealing with Korean people. I love Korean food, but if I cook that way, I'm just under the microscope of Korean people, and that's like the worst fucking thing. Koreans are gonna bitch about the spices, everyone's going to say this is not how it's made, my grandmother made it this way and, honestly, I don't need that.

**Let's talk about your chef friends, your colleagues in the cooking community around the country. A lot of cooks are experimenting and really making an effort to use Korean products. We have an entire chapter of examples in this book (see Respect: Guest Recipes). Are you finding any of your friends using Korean flavors in a cool way that is worth mentioning?**

The person who's doing something really cool with Korean food is Corey Lee [of Benu in San Francisco]. And he doesn't even do that much Korean food. Gochujang is great, and I want to incorporate different versions of that in the mainstream. I want it to be like sriracha. But there's also a part of me that feels it's weird to see kimchi on so many non-Asian menus. The best analogy I can give is that everyone's treating Korean food like 3-D movies. Like, for the past couple of years, everything had to be 3-D. And now no one gives a shit about 3-D.

**What do you think of Korean restaurants these days?**

A lot of Korean food just isn't made properly with really good ingredients, and that's sort of what inspired our bossam. I was like, why does it have to suck? But, in general, there are classic flavors that work together. Pork and kimchi, for example. But there are lots of real Korean flavors that just don't speak to me. And they rarely speak to the mainstream population.

Just think about real Chinese food. For years, people have been going to China and coming back to say, "Oh, the food's terrible." Guys, the food hasn't changed in fucking five hundred years! It's just that the people (in the United States) are eating fucking bland, Americanized Chinese food here, and they get the real thing [in China], and they're like, "Oh it sucks." And it's similar with Korean food. Kimchi by nature is offensive, and there's no other food on the planet that better represents the culture of Koreans than kimchi. Korean food is just a little bit more rustic, a little bit more hardcore. And you know, that's why I avoid restaurants that try to take the guts out of Korean food. You just can't make Korean food look nice.

**And that's why I personally love it so much. Korean food has all these rough edges, but then you see photos of it in soft focus and it looks so pretty and prissy.**

It's tough. There are a lot of ways I would make Korean food better. I have a complicated relationship with Korean food, man. It's something I want to do, but there's something that keeps me from really embracing it as something that's pristine. And I think that I can still make it look like Korean food, but make it better.

**Well, start by making your own gochujang and doenjang. More people need to do that.**

More people do need to do that! And more people need to make their own ssamjang for barbecue. You make all that shit from scratch, and it's amazingly good. I mean, the reason why L.A. Korean food is better than Seoul is because the ingredients are better.

**Give me an example?**

To me, the place that does spicy chicken off Olympic in Koreatown, Mapo Galbi, is one of, if not my favorite restaurant in the world right now. Because the woman there is cooking her ass off. You start off with the chicken in its raw state, and as you cook it on the grill, it changes. It becomes a little bit sweeter, then a little bit spicier, and you see a transformation from raw to cooked to overcooked—in a variety of textures and bitterness. It's making something very simple, very complex. But no one would see this small Korean restaurant as being really complex, unless you really wanna look at it. And there's no bullshit to it, and that's what I like.

**It drives me crazy when people say Korean food is simple. I mean, just making kimchi and the jangs takes several weeks. Several months, you know.**

It's a lot of work. You know, Korean food is a weird thing, man. It's just a highly neurotic cuisine. There's no other food that is loved and hated at the same time by the people who adore it the most.

# This Is How You Make Shin Ramyun
## 신라면
### THE BEST INSTANT RAMYUN ON EARTH

Shin (which means "spicy" in Korean) is by far the most popular instant ramyun (Korean parlance for ramen) in South Korea and is eaten throughout the world. First introduced to the market in 1986, over 22 billion bags have been sold in over eighty countries. It is said that, on average, South Koreans eat seventy bags per person annually, which is a hell of a lot of instant noodles. With this, finding a consensus recipe for preparing the perfect bowl of Shin has proven impossible. What we do know is that following the standard package instructions is never OK just on its own. Possible additions include eggs, fish cakes, bok choy, American cheese, hot dogs, scallions, mushrooms, tofu and sriracha. These are all great ideas. Here is our way, which elevates the broth with the richness of egg and American cheese because . . . America! We also stand behind a fanning technique that we think creates the ideal texture for the noodles. **SERVES 1**

2½ cups water

1 4.2-ounce package of Shin Ramyun Noodle Soup (includes noodles, vegetable mix and soup base)

1 egg

1 slice of American or Cheddar cheese

Special equipment:
1 paper fan

1  Bring 2½ cups of water to a boil in a large saucepan over high heat. Add the soup base and vegetable mix from the ramyun package. Boil for 1 minute.

2  Add the whole block of noodle. *Do not break the noodles in half!* This is crucial. Submerge them in the boiling water with chopsticks or a fork. Once the noodles have softened, in about 2 minutes, lift the noodles out of the broth with chopsticks and fan them repeatedly for 2 minutes. (The lid for the pot will do.) The flow of air will stunt the noodles' cooking process, giving them a more al dente texture, which we can all agree is the best way to eat noodles. Yeah?

3  Place the noodles back in the boiling soup. Crack the egg and add it to the noodles. Cover the pot and boil for 30 seconds. Turn off the heat. Add the slice of cheese and re-cover for 30 seconds so the cheese melts. Serve immediately.

# EATING KOREATOWN
## LINKIN PARK DJ JOE HAHN

We're in the North Hollywood studio of Linkin Park, the acclaimed band that has sold over 60 million albums. A plate of jokbal from Jang Choong Dong sits in front of the band's DJ and producer, Joe Hahn, and he's waving his hands with excitement. He's getting amped talking about Korean food.

Hahn grew up in Los Angeles and was surrounded by the city's proud and vibrant Korean community. "There was always a jar of kimchi, always a jar of doenjang, which, if you don't know, smells pretty delicious," he says with a laugh. We get to talking about the joys of a spicy vegetable and noodle dish that brings tears to the eyes, both due to spice and sentiment. "My mom used to make bibimmyeon for me, and it always reminded me that I was home."

This brings us to a point that millions of Korean Americans likely have grappled with: homesickness. Whether they moved here from Korea or are trying to make their way in a society where Koreans are a tiny minority, longing for the foods they grew up on is a common experience. And Hahn can certainly relate, as a touring musician who is asked to live on a bus for weeks at a time. "While on tour we would be in an RV or bus with a microwave, and I'd get this microwaveable rice and add soy sauce and dried seaweed as a reminder of home," says Hahn. "But it sure as hell beats Waffle House."

Naturally, when talking with a guy who plays his share of late-night club dates, we hit the topic of eating Korean food after hours. "Sometimes I will crave jjampong, this spicy seafood soup, but you have to know where to find it. And sometimes, you can't," he says. But he's learned one way to deal when hunger and nostalgia strike while on tour. "Sometimes it's as simple as a package of Shin ramyun." In the tour bus with him, always, is a supply of his favorite Korean instant noodles.

# Jjajangmyeon

## 자장면

### BLACK BEAN NOODLES

While Koreans obviously love noodles, the cuisine is slightly less noodle-focused than that of East Asian neighbors China and Japan. But Jjajangmyeon is here to save the freaking day (blow your freaking mind). It's mild, salty and unites pork fat with a Korean black bean paste called chunjang. Like the greasy takeout lo mein that everyone loves, these noodles should be slightly oily and splatter a little when slurped. And if you can't find fresh noodles, you can substitute instant ramyun (minus the spice packet) or even spaghetti.

And fun fact—well, slightly depressing fun fact: Jjajangmyeon is typically eaten on what Koreans call Black Day, which is observed every April 14. The idea is that those who didn't receive a gift on February 14 (Valentine's Day) or March 14 (White Day, when girls return the favor to the boys)—should treat themselves to a bowl of black noodles and commiserate on their life of perpetual singledom. SERVES 4 TO 6 PEOPLE

1 Bring a large pot of water to a boil and add the noodles. Boil the noodles for 8 minutes, until soft (just beyond al dente), reserve 1½ cups of the noodle cooking water and drain and rinse the noodles with cold water to cool to room temperature. Drain well and reserve.

2 While the noodles are boiling, heat the oil on high heat in a wok or large skillet until lightly smoking. Add diced pork belly and shoulder and render for 2 minutes.

3 Add ginger and garlic and sauté for 1 minute, being mindful not to let it burn. Add carrots, potatoes, onions and diced zucchini and sauté for 6 minutes, until the vegetables are softened.

4 Mix in the black bean paste, sugar, 1 cup of reserved noodle water and salt to taste. Cook for 7 minutes, or until the sauce has thickened and the potatoes are cooked. If necessary, add more noodle water to keep it moist.

5 Divide noodles into bowls and top with warm sauce. Garnish with julienned zucchini and pickled yellow daikon.

---

1 pound fresh jjajangmyeon or udon noodles (or substitute a couple packages of instant ramen noodles)

2 tablespoons vegetable oil

6 ounces fatty pork belly, cut into large dice

3 ounces pork shoulder, cut into large dice

1-inch knob of ginger, minced

2 garlic cloves, minced

½ medium carrot, diced

1 large Yukon Gold potato, peeled and cut into small dice

2 medium red onions, diced

½ zucchini, peeled and diced, plus ¼ cup julienned zucchini

½ cup black bean paste (chunjang)

2 tablespoons sugar

Kosher salt to taste

¼ pickled yellow daikon, cut into half-moons (optional)

½ pound of pork fat trimmings or fatty pork belly, roughly chopped

1 cup water

2 garlic cloves, minced

¼ cup coarsely ground gochugaru

1 tablespoon kosher salt

1 teaspoon black pepper

4 cups Anchovy Stock (page 195)

¼ cup thinly sliced zucchini

¼ cup thinly sliced carrots

1 small onion, cut into medium dice

¼ pound mussels in shell

¼ pound head-on shrimp

¼ pound baby octopus or squid

¼ pound scallops

1 package (2 servings) fresh udon noodles

Soy sauce to taste

# Jjampong
# 짬뽕

## SPICY SEAFOOD NOODLE SOUP

This seafood noodle soup gets its craveable identity from pork fat, lots of briny seafood (mussels, scallops, head-on shrimp) and a nice handful of gochugaru. We cannot name a more satisfying dish that is slept on by non-Koreans.

You'll be shocked by how easy it is to make a large pot of the broth, which keeps well in the refrigerator and can last for a couple of days of leftovers. Korean udon noodles are typically bought fresh and found in the cooler at any Asian supermarket; they can be boiled directly in the soup. Also keep in mind that using a decent amount of fatty pork trimmings or belly gives the dish a distinct porkiness, but if you want to hold off, it's all good. Any of the seafood components can be substituted for one another. If the baby octopus isn't as fresh as you want, skip it and add more head-on shrimp (the head is where all the flavor is).

SERVES 2

1 Add the diced pork fat and 1 cup water to a small saucepan over medium-low heat and bring to a vigorous simmer. Simmer for 5 minutes. Strain out trimmings and reserve liquid. (Meat can be reserved and used for another purpose.)

2 In a bowl, combine the garlic, gochugaru, salt, pepper and the reserved pork broth. Set aside.

3 In a medium soup pot, combine the garlic mixture (from step 2) with the Anchovy Stock, zucchini, carrots, onions, mussels, shrimp, octopus, scallops and udon noodles. Bring to a boil over high heat, then lower heat and simmer for 5 minutes, or until the mussels have opened, the noodles and seafood are cooked, and the stew has turned a deep red and acquired a rich seafood flavor. Season to taste with soy sauce.

# CHICAGO
## MOTT STREET

"Do you call yourself a Korean chef?" The question hangs in the air while a Robot Coupe whirs in the background. We're sitting in the dining room of Mott Street, the well-regarded Korean (but also Chinese, Vietnamese and Midwesternese) restaurant in Chicago's Wicker Park neighborhood. It's three hours before a busy weekend service, and the scene is controlled chaos.

At the bar, bartenders are road testing a new cocktail menu, with coupes and shakers filled with exotic citrus and Letherbee Gin scattered about. At a small table, the waitstaff are being briefed by a wine rep going over his portfolio. In the back, a young cook is methodically portioning out the night's stuffed kimchi, pork shoulder and rice "lasagna" (see page 221). As for the question? It's posed to the restaurant's ever-calm, clairvoyant leader, chef-owner Edward Kim, who sits at a table situated in the center of the commotion.

"This can of worms has to be opened," he says, soothingly, in a medium-strength Chicago accent. "I'm obviously Korean, obviously Korean American and obviously very proud of it. It's a huge influence on the food that I make. It's the food that my mother, father and grandmother made."

Yet the food at Mott Street, and the restaurant that put the Chicago native on the map, Ruxbin, isn't bibimbap. There's crab fried rice, which utilizes the crustacean's best briny bits with a nice amount of Chinese sausage and lime—as well as crispy chicken wings glazed with the union of soy, jaggery sugar and two types of dried chiles, and then tossed with sesame, poppy seeds,

fried shallots and a tzatziki dipping sauce. It's as if an everything bagel booked a first-class trip around the world. If food can be called the great equalizer—bringing different cultures together around a common table—the menu of Mott Street positions Kim as a sort of UN secretary-general.

"The Chicago palate has so much acid in it," says the chef when asked about how the flavors of Asia are embraced by his Midwestern clientele. "Take the deep-dish pizza and the salad placed atop the hot dogs here. Growing up I was drawn to that as much as I was drawn to kimchi, which is why Korean flavors have been accepted."

To answer the original question, Mott Street is an American restaurant through and through; the chef even sources doenjang from Doalnara Organic Farm in Tennessee. And in the year 2016, food in America is as diverse as ever. "One of the beauties is that there are so many cultures here," he says smiling. "Sambal, A-1, gochujang—it can all go into the same dish." And we have no doubt Kim will do that one day, and the result will be creative, technically sound and, most important, delicious.

3 cups all-purpose flour, plus more for rolling

1 cup water

1 tablespoon vegetable oil

1 tablespoon kosher salt

1 pound littleneck clams, scrubbed clean

8 cups Anchovy Stock (page 195)

1 cup medium-dice carrots

1 cup peeled medium-dice zucchini

1 cup peeled medium-dice russet potatoes

1 garlic clove, minced

2 tablespoons soy sauce, plus more to taste

1 scallion, sliced into 2-inch batons, for garnish

# Kalguksu
## 칼국수
### KNIFE-CUT NOODLE SOUP

Kalguksu ("knife-cut noodles") is sometimes called Korean fettuccine and is served most commonly with shellfish (one of our favorites is prepared with littleneck clams). The broth is clean and refined, made with our simple Anchovy Stock (page 195), and a simple DIY noodle recipe can be rolled out on your countertop in little time. Although it's counterintuitive to some people, boiling bowls of kalguksu are eaten more often in the summer. The idea is that the hot soup gives one energy when slurped after a day running around in the heat. We're not going to debate hundreds of years of tradition, but we'll eat this in the middle of January as well. SERVES 4 TO 6

1 In a large bowl, use a fork to stir together flour, 1 cup of water, vegetable oil and salt and mix until it forms a dough; knead it in the bowl for about 5 minutes. If the dough is too sticky, add a dusting of flour. The dough should form a smooth ball. Cover with plastic wrap and refrigerate for 1 hour.

2 While the dough rests, cover the clams with cold water and set aside.

3 Remove the dough from the refrigerator, turn it onto a lightly floured work surface and pat it out into a rectangle. With a rolling pin, roll the dough very thin ($1/10$ inch) and dust it lightly with flour. Fold the dough into thirds, first from the bottom to the middle then from the top to the middle. Dust lightly with flour. With a knife, cut the dough into ¼-inch-wide noodles. Divide the noodles into 4 or 6 servings, and twirl each serving into a loose knot, adding a dusting of flour to keep the bundles from sticking together. Set aside.

4 In a large pot, bring the Anchovy Stock to a boil over high heat. Add carrots, zucchini and potatoes and boil for about 8 minutes, until the carrots and potatoes are just about done. Carefully remove the clams from the cold water, leaving any grit behind in the bowl. Add clams and noodles to the stock and simmer for 2 minutes, or until the clams open and the noodles are just cooked but still chewy. Remove from the heat and add garlic and soy sauce to taste. Divide into bowls, garnish with scallions and serve immediately.

# Jaengban Guksu
## 쟁반 국수
### SPICY COLD BUCKWHEAT NOODLES

There are three main components to this wonderfully spicy cold noodle dish: chilled buckwheat noodles, a load of chopped vegetables and herbs and a tangy sauce that brings it all together. It's a great example of how Korean cooking can be light and low impact (healthy!) while still being interesting and delicious. We like to make a large platter to share on a hot summer night, which for many Koreans is the season to eat lots and lots of cold noodles like Kongguksu (page 87) and Dongchimi Guksu (see page 45). The vegetable prep can take a while—you'll thank yourself for investing in that mandoline slicer—but it can be done in advance, as can the sauce that blends sweetness from the apples and pears and a nice amount of spice (kind of like chojang, but with less vinegar). For the buckwheat noodles, Japanese soba will work great, and they should be cooked to order and shocked in ice water just before serving, to give you the ideal al dente consistency. You will notice the addition of mugwort (ssuk in Korean), which is a medicinal herb with a peppery flavor that is sometimes pureed and folded into rice cakes. If you cannot find mugwort, we suggest substituting arugula. SERVES 2

1  Bring a large pot of water to a boil over high heat. Set up a bowl of ice water nearby.

2  Add the ½ Asian pear and the apple to a blender and puree until smooth.

3  In a medium bowl, combine the puree along with gochujang, syrup, gochugaru, sugar, soy sauce, mirin, garlic, black pepper and toasted sesame seeds to make the sauce.

4  Cook the noodles as directed on the package. Shock in ice water, then drain and reserve.

5  Divide the cold noodles between 2 plates. Add half the vegetables, herbs and sliced pear to each plate, along with 2 tablespoons of the sauce. Top with a halved soft-boiled egg. Serve artfully arranged or mixed together. Add more sauce as needed; leftover sauce keeps 3 days, refrigerated.

½ Asian pear, peeled and cored, plus ½ cup thinly sliced

1 apple, Gala or Fuji, peeled and cored

½ cup gochujang

¼ cup Korean rice or corn syrup

2 tablespoons finely ground gochugaru

2 tablespoons sugar

2 tablespoons soy sauce

1 tablespoon mirin

2 garlic cloves, minced

1 teaspoon black pepper

1 tablespoon toasted sesame seeds

6 ounces dried buckwheat noodles

½ cup shredded red cabbage

½ cup thinly sliced cucumbers

½ cup thinly sliced carrots

½ cup thinly sliced red or white onions

½ cup mugwort leaves

½ cup perilla leaves, thinly sliced

¼ cup bean sprouts

2 eggs, soft-boiled

2 cups roughly chopped green cabbage

2-inch knob of ginger, minced

4 garlic cloves, minced

2 pounds ground pork (80 percent lean)

1 tablespoon kosher salt

1 pound (4 sticks) unsalted butter, cut into chunks and softened to room temperature

45 refrigerated or frozen and thawed round Asian dumpling wrappers

Fresh Napa Cabbage Kimchi (page 41), for serving

Light soy sauce, for serving

Vegetable or sesame oil, as needed (optional, for panfrying)

# Butter Mandu
# 버터만두
## BUTTER DUMPLINGS

Pretty much every culture has their version of a dumpling. Why? Because wrapping flavorful things in a pouch of dough is just a really great idea. We're looking at you, Ashkenazi kreplach, Russian pelmeni, Japanese gyoza and goose-liver ravioli from the kingdom of Mario Batali. If you make your way up to Koreatown in New York City, you'll find a longtime favorite, Mandoo Bar, located in a small storefront in the heart of 32nd Street. From the street you can watch the old women rolling and stuffing from morning until night. In Los Angeles, mandu is supreme at Pao Jao Dumpling House, located in the basement food court of Koreatown Plaza at the corner of San Marino Street and Western Avenue. And at the Buford Highway Farmers Market in Doraville, Georgia, mandu is made daily.

This recipe comes from Deuki's father and has origins in North Korea, the ancestral home of mandu. (Sharing a border with China, it is no coincidence that *mandu* sounds a lot like the Chinese word for steamed bread, *mantou*.) Instead of the versions stuffed with finely chopped kimchi, Deuki grew up eating mandu with kimchi on the side. The star in this recipe is the very generous quantity of butter, which is mixed in with the pork, garlic and ginger and adds a real-deal richness to each bite. Not typically used in East Asian cooking, butter is a fully Americanized, fully awesome way to rethink the mandu. SERVES 4 TO 6

1 Place the cabbage, ginger and garlic in the bowl of a food processor and pulse until finely chopped. Place the cabbage mixture in a large bowl.

2 Using your hands, fold the ground pork into the cabbage mixture just enough to combine. Evenly sprinkle it with the salt and fold it in. Gently fold the butter into the mixture until thoroughly combined.

3 To assemble the mandu, place about 2 tablespoons of the filling in the center of each wrapper. Be careful not to overfill or the filling could leak while cooking. (If your wrappers are small, decrease the amount of filling per dumpling; the mandu should be full but not hard to close.) Dip your fingertip in a glass of water and paint the edge of

the wrapper. Fold the wrapper over to form a half-moon and pinch the edges together to seal. (This is the easiest fold, for simplicity's sake, but you can fold your mandu in a number of fancy ways, like the pros do.) Mandu can be cooked right away or frozen for later (see below).

4 **TO STEAM:** In a large pot, bring a few cups of water to a boil over high heat and insert a lightly oiled steaming basket above the water; do not submerge it. Carefully place the dumplings in the basket in one layer. Cover and steam for 5 to 7 minutes, or until the wrapper is a little translucent and the filling feels firm. Serve immediately with kimchi and soy sauce.

**TO FRY:** Coat a sauté pan with some vegetable or sesame oil and place over medium heat. When the oil is shimmering-hot, place the fresh or thawed mandu in the pan, just enough to fit comfortably in one layer, and sauté each side for a few minutes until golden brown and cooked through. Serve with kimchi and soy sauce.

1 pound long-fermented Napa Cabbage Kimchi (page 41), roughly chopped

8 ounces firm tofu, squeezed through cheesecloth to remove excess water

3 scallions, thinly sliced

1 medium onion, minced

2 garlic cloves, minced

1 teaspoon minced ginger

3 tablespoons coarsely ground gochugaru

1 tablespoon kosher salt

45 refrigerated or frozen and thawed round Asian dumpling wrappers

Vegetable oil, as needed (optional, for panfrying)

Fresh kimchi, for serving

Light soy sauce, for serving

# Mukeunji Kimchi Mandu
## 묵은지만두
### AGED KIMCHI DUMPLINGS

Because not everybody is in the mood for butter and pork (we aren't judging), we wanted to do a vegetable dumpling that was *high impact*. For serious flavor, we decided to go with long-fermented napa cabbage kimchi, called mukeunji. As the name suggests, this is the kimchi that has been aging for months, up to a year in some cases. It's sharp and slightly fizzy on the tongue. It packs a punch, and we love using it in dumplings. You can find older kimchi in all Korean grocery stores, but you may need to ask somebody to point you in the right direction as the labeling is typically written in Korean only. And if you only have younger kimchi, you can set it out at room temperature for a day or so to get a little more of that mature flavor. SERVES 4 TO 8

1 Combine all ingredients, except for dumpling wrappers, vegetable oil, fresh kimchi and soy sauce, in a food processor and pulse until finely chopped.

2 To assemble the mandu, place about 2 tablespoons of the filling in the center of each wrapper. Be careful not to overfill, or the filling could leak while cooking. (If your wrappers are small, decrease the amount of filling per dumpling; the mandu should be full but not hard to close.) Dip your fingertip in a glass of water and paint the edge of the wrapper. Fold the wrapper over to form a half-moon and pinch the edges together to seal. Mandu can be cooked right away, or frozen for later (see below).

3 **TO STEAM:** In a large pot, bring a few cups of water to a boil over high heat and insert a lightly oiled steaming basket above the water; do not submerge. Carefully place the dumplings in the basket. If frozen, you can just chuck them in. Cover and steam for 5 minutes, or until the wrapper is a little translucent and the filling feels firm. Serve immediately with fresh kimchi and light soy sauce.

**TO FRY:** Coat a sauté pan with some oil and place over medium heat. When the oil is shimmering-hot, place fresh or thawed mandu in the pan, just enough to fit comfortably in one layer, and sauté each side for a few minutes until golden brown and hot throughout. Serve with fresh kimchi and light soy sauce.

# Barbecue:
# Grilled, Smoked
# & Fired

## 바베큐

The Long Island Railroad is a major artery linking Manhattan with the suburban sprawl of Queens and Long Island. One of those Queens communities, Murray Hill, is just a twenty-minute ride from midtown Manhattan, but it's a world away. Exiting the train is like stepping onto a Gyeongbu Line platform in South Korea. All around are shops and storefronts emblazoned with Hangul advertising Korean-owned accountants, salons and pool halls. There are also some very good restaurants in this quiet Korean village. But a short walk down 149th Place, and your nose will take you to the promised land.

Mapo BBQ is a throwback, famous for its charcoal grills and mastery of beef short ribs, kalbi. The secret—aside from the quality of the meat and the soy sauce, garlic and Asian pear marinade—is the grill itself. The lion's share of Korean barbecue in America is cooked over gas. It's safer (at least according to some city officials) and more "modern," at least to the untrained eye. Charcoal is dirty business, and after eating in a place like Mapo, you really feel like you've been playing a role in the cooking process. Well, at least your smoked-out cardigan will tell you that (though at Mapo and lots of other charcoal restaurants, you can check your jackets and sweaters in garment bags at the door). But given the result, it's all worth it. Charcoal offers a smoky flavor, and its higher heat rewards with a better char.

We're not going to blame you if you've skipped directly to this chapter. It's a universally loved food and what many people relate to when they think of Korean food. Unlike American-style barbecue—the low-and-slow methods of Texas and North Carolina—Korean barbecue is actually a form of grilling: cuts of short ribs, brisket and pork belly are brought out raw and cooked at the center of the table. This is the typical practice in both Korean restaurants and within Korean homes, where portable gas grills are considered a member of the family.

And, happily, Korean barbecue is really easy to make, and the ingredients are easy to find at pretty much any grocery store—whether it's called Hanahreum Market or Kroger. 고기

# HOW TO COOK KOREAN FOOD AT HOME
# WITHOUT PISSING OFF YOUR NEIGHBORS

With the very smart decision to cook Korean food comes a level of responsibility. With highly fermented kimchis and dishes with names like "dead body soup" (don't worry, no dead bodies appear within these pages), Korean home cooking can sometimes draw the ire of sensitive-nosed neighbors, especially if you live in tightly packed apartments like we do. But this shouldn't stop you from diving into these pages headfirst. Well, nose first. For city dwellers, here are some tips for cooking the recipes from this book while staying on good terms with the condo board.

## 1. CONTROL THE FUNKINESS

Sure, the most intense Korean ingredients like kimchi and doenjang can make their presence felt like an awkward freshman-year roommate. In fact, in many Korean homes, certain ingredients are quarantined in a separate refrigerator. But for those without a dedicated kimchi fridge, here are a few simple solutions:

**Turkey Oven Bags** This little trick is normally employed by weed dealers. (Not that we know anything about that.) Store opened jars of kimchi and any of the deeply fermented jangs in sealed oven bags to contain the odor. Are you lucky enough to get your hands on a package of one-year aged kimchi? You might as well double bag it. If it can mask the scent of Sour Diesel, it should handle pickled cabbage with no problems.

**Coffee Grounds** Place a container of dry coffee grounds in the back of your fridge to help get rid of any funky smells. We tried the open box of baking soda, and, well, it did nothing. But the coffee trick works, especially when you replace it occasionally to maintain a fresh scent.

**Activated Charcoal** You can purchase odor eliminators like Fridge It or opt for charcoal purchased in pet-supply shops. Spread the latter in a bowl or half-size sheet tray and store it on the bottom shelf of the refrigerator until smells are neutralized.

## 2. BE MINDFUL OF THE SMOKE KOREAN COOKING CAN CAUSE

Unless your home kitchen is tricked out with an industrial exhaust hood (like the ones found in restaurant kitchens), Korean barbecue is best cooked on an outdoor charcoal grill. But should weather or space pose an issue, your next best option is to use an indoor propane grill, or a blazing hot cast-iron grill pan. Before anything hits the pan, drain as much marinade off the meat as possible. Otherwise, you'll burn the sugars.

But even if you're mindful of the marinade situation, it's always a good idea to open windows because nothing ruins dinner quite like the shrill screams of a smoke detector. Finally, we ask that you avoid cooking with any boxer-endorsed panini presses and other appliances of that ilk. They will never reach the sizzling temperatures necessary for achieving the grill marks and flavor that are expected of great barbecue.

Ultimately, Korean food oftentimes reveals serious aroma as it's being cooked: it's called *flavor!* So really, your best bet is to invite the neighbors over to taste whatever it is that they can smell in the halls.

¼ cup diced fresh or canned pineapple

½ onion, roughly chopped

1 Asian pear, peeled, cored and chopped

1 apple, peeled, cored and chopped

6 garlic cloves

1 cup soy sauce

5 tablespoons sesame oil

½ cup sugar

¼ cup mirin

¼ cup sake

4 cups water

4 pounds short ribs, thinly sliced (butterflied) ½ to ¼ inch thick (see Note, page 176)

Vegetable oil, as needed for pan-searing (optional)

**FOR SERVING**

4 cups hot cooked rice

1 head red leaf lettuce, leaves washed, separated and dried

5 to 10 perilla leaves (optional)

1 cup Napa Cabbage Kimchi (page 41), or other kimchi of your choice

1 cup Ssamjang (page 115)

# Kalbi

## 갈비

### MARINATED SHORT RIBS

The beefy short rib is one of the most prized cuts in the Korean barbecue spectrum. In American restaurants, the cut is typically flanken—meaning cut across the bone, about ½ inch thick. This is called L.A. kalbi, which some say refers to the city where many Korean immigrants settled in the 1970s and '80s. You can find fresh or frozen short ribs precut in the L.A. style at all Korean grocery stores. But for the sake of this recipe, any ½- to ¼-inch-thick cut of short ribs will serve you right.

The marinade is light and sweetened with apples and pears. We also like to use fresh pineapple, which has an enzyme called bromelain that acts as a natural tenderizer. It's best to let all Korean beef marinades, including this one, sit a day in the refrigerator before soaking the meat for a half to full day. This allows the soy sauce, sugars, fruits and vegetables to mingle in the most magical way. It's how Deuki does it at his Manhattan restaurant and most certainly worth the extra time.

Once grilled, kalbi is usually wrapped in lettuce or perilla leaves, packed with a bite of rice, kimchi and the savory barbecue paste called ssamjang. You can buy it in the store, but our homemade recipe on page 115 is pretty much the truth. SERVES 6 TO 8

1 **PREPARE THE MARINADE:** In a blender or food processor, combine the pineapple, onion, Asian pear, apple and garlic and puree until smooth.

2 In a large bowl, combine the puree with the soy sauce, sesame oil, sugar, mirin, sake and the water. If you have the time, refrigerate the marinade for a day on its own. Add the short ribs and let marinate for at least 12 and up to 24 hours, in the fridge.

3 Remove the meat from the marinade and pat dry.

4 **TO PAN-SEAR THE MEAT:** Preheat a large cast-iron skillet or grill pan, greased with a tablespoon of vegetable oil, over high heat until smoking hot. Working in batches, grill the marinated beef in one layer until cooked through, about 5 minutes, turning frequently until the meat begins to caramelize. Serve the meat as it is ready. Using kitchen shears, cut the meat into bite-sized pieces.

**TO GRILL THE MEAT:** Preheat a charcoal or gas grill on medium-high; you should be able to hold your hand 6 inches above the grill grate for only 3 to 4 seconds before you need to pull it away. Working in batches that fit comfortably in one layer, grill the short ribs until browned, about 3 minutes on each side. Using kitchen shears, cut the ribs into bite-sized pieces.

5 Serve the ribs with the rice, lettuce, perilla, kimchi and Ssamjang alongside. To eat, make a lettuce wrap (called ssambap): take a lettuce or perilla leaf in your palm and pack on a couple spoons of rice. Layer with kimchi and a piece of short ribs and top with a dab of Ssamjang.

# EATING KOREATOWN
## KOREAN FOOD NUT ANDREW ZIMMERN

"Korean food is my all-time favorite, and it's ready for its bright, shiny moment," says TV food personality and samgyeopsal fanatic Andrew Zimmern at dinner in Minneapolis. "There are certain Korean dishes that you try and you just cannot help but fall in love with, and Americans are now just starting to find out about them," Zimmern continues. He points out wisely that the Japanese ramen craze hasn't done anything but help Korean food climb the Asian food ladder. "Korean cuisine has a deep soup culture, with all the various guks and jjigaes and everything in between, and now the American consumer is ready for the full monty of Korean food."

Zimmern acknowledges that consumers have recognized the formulaic barbecue experience and have started looking to chefs like Chris Shepherd (Houston) and Hooni Kim (New York City) to push boundaries, but he finds that, for many, there is still a steep learning curve with Korean cuisine.

"I was out at a barbecue restaurant with a bunch of famous chefs, and nobody wanted to order," says Zimmern of a late-night trip to New Wonjo in New York City. "Nobody knew how to order! One of them, and this is a really smart guy, told me that they were sick and tired of ordering the same *three* dishes. One of them told me they were once given marinated raw crab and didn't know what to do. They wanted me to save them." Lesson: Even professional food people are still just starting their adventures in Korean food.

So how can they best learn? One kind of answer may be found in the restaurant we're sitting in: the Rabbit Hole. It's a genius name for a modern Korean restaurant, a kitchen with one eye on traditional pojang-macha cooking—like ddeokbokki cooked with duck fat—and another eye on the crowd-pleasing crossover fare that plays well with the kalbi-and-potatoes Minneapolis population. Gochugaru flourless cake anyone?

# Ssamjang
## 쌈장

### THE GREAT KOREAN BARBECUE CONDIMENT

Given that this is a barbecue chapter, this is sort of required reading. Ssamjang is the crimson-brown spread you will find on the table at Korean barbecue restaurants. For some back-of-the-napkin etymology, *ssam* means "wrapped," and *jang* means "thick sauce," so by definition this is a spread to be slathered on lettuce or perilla leaves that are then wrapped around the hunks of grilled meat, kimchi and any of the banchan you want to include. It's a warhorse of a condiment. The flavor of ssamjang is complex and layered, something we have trouble describing. In fact, we sat around the test kitchen for a good fifteen minutes throwing out words like *umami*, *sweet* and *nutty* before simply settling on *essential*. That is, all Korean barbecue tables need a home-made version.

Commercial ssamjang is widely available in Korean markets (it's the green plastic tub in the jangs aisle). It's not bad, and it's what you will find served at the larger Korean barbecue restaurants. But like many condiments in the Korean kitchen, a homemade version is fuller in flavor. Ssamjang also makes a killer dip for raw vegetables like carrots and celery. **MAKES ABOUT 1 CUP**

**Mix all ingredients in a bowl and serve. Store in an airtight container. Will keep, refrigerated, up to one month.**

**5 tablespoons doenjang**

**3½ tablespoons gochujang**

**2 garlic cloves, minced**

**1 tablespoon sliced scallions**

**1 tablespoon minced onions**

**1 tablespoon sesame oil**

**1 tablespoon sesame seeds**

**1½ tablespoons Korean rice or corn syrup**

**2 tablespoons walnuts, coarsely chopped**

# GAS VS. CHARCOAL

As reliable as the seasons and the Chicago Cubs' playoff impotence, every Memorial Day brings the great gas versus charcoal debate—disputed within the pages of your favorite food magazine and by a tong-wielding Al Roker on the *Today* show. Gas, as some grill masters put it, is ideal for superior temperature control and overall simplicity. Set it to high, medium or low, and it's like the outdoor version of your oven. Charcoal, on the other hand, is all about variable (and extreme) heat and flavor—imparting a true smokiness to your meat and vegetables. There are many arguments for each side, with no clear winner.

---

The same most certainly cannot be said for Korean barbecue restaurants. Charcoal, as any kalbi geek will tell you, is hands down superior. It's also a dying art form that you have to seek out. Long before building inspectors and health departments regulated American restaurants with the vigilance of the Capitol forces in the *Hunger Games*, charcoal was how people ate Korean barbecue. Part of it was economics: charcoal, smoldering around the clock inside furnaces in a restaurant's basement, is far cheaper than installing gas lines or investing in tabletop grills fueled by propane canisters. But more than a money issue, charcoal means flavor. A hotter fire awards a better char and a light smokiness. It's certainly not the smokiness caused by the low-and-slow effects of burning hardwood—that would be American barbecue, a beautiful topic unto itself—but the enhanced flavor of a real Korean charcoal experience is still noticeable.

Gas, on the other hand, is what it is—an efficient and safe heat source that can be controlled by a single switch (and no wonder why gas is widely required for new barbecue establishments). On the contrary, dining at a charcoal barbecue restaurant can be . . . an adventure, or even slightly dangerous! After a barbecue order is placed, the server notifies the brave staff member tasked with bringing the "hot box" to the table, oftentimes navigating a busy dining room packed with the drunk and disorderly. Note: Tip the hot-box guy. He deserves it.

Once at the table, the charcoal is dumped into the communal grill, possibly singeing a few arm hairs in the process (you're too hungry and excited to think about lawsuits at that point). Your face is warmed by a heat that is unexpectedly intense—unlike anything you have ever felt in a restaurant in your life. Once the grill reaches it optimal heat, the server will start to layer the strips of meat atop the intense fire. And before you take another swig of OB, the blistering hot meat is ready for the lettuce wrap. Gas just isn't the same.

With new building codes, though, charcoal barbecue restaurants are an endangered species and quickly going the way of Chi-Chi's. Few remain, and here are some of our favorites around the country:

**Seo Ra Beol** 3040 Steve Reynolds Boulevard, Duluth, Georgia 30096; 770-497-1155
**Mapo BBQ** 149-24 41st Ave., Flushing, New York 11355; 718-886-8292
**Soot Bull Jeep** 3136 West 8th Street, Los Angeles, California 90005; 213-387-3865

1 cup soy sauce

1 large white onion,
grated

¼ cup sugar

2 tablespoons mirin

8 garlic cloves, minced

1 tablespoon sesame oil

2 tablespoons black
pepper

2 pounds rib eye or
sirloin, very thinly sliced

4 scallions, cut into
1-inch batons

1 tablespoon sesame
seeds

Vegetable oil, as needed

FOR SERVING

4 cups hot cooked rice

1 head red leaf lettuce,
leaves washed,
separated and dried

5 to 10 perilla leaves
(optional)

1 cup Napa Cabbage
Kimchi (page 41), or
other kimchi of your
choice

1 cup Ssamjang
(page 115)

# Bulgogi
## 불고기
### SOY-MARINATED GRILLED RIB EYE

Next to kimchi, and possibly bibimbap, bulgogi is the best-known Korean food product to grace American shores. Thinly sliced beef, usually sirloin, rib eye or brisket, is marinated in a mixture of soy sauce, mirin and sesame oil before landing on a smoking-hot grill or grill pan—or a tableside grill, if you want your house to smell like the magic of Koreatown. Although kalbi is more coveted, and thus expensive, bulgogi is really the workhorse of Korean barbecue. It's what Roy Choi placed in a taco to start a culinary revolution. Any good Korean grocery store will sell presliced beef for this recipe. This is the best bet, but you can do it yourself: freeze the meat for about 20 minutes so it's stiff enough to shave with a sharp knife. Or you can ask your butcher to slice it for you. SERVES 4

1 **PREPARE THE MARINADE:** In a bowl, stir together the soy sauce, onion, sugar, mirin, garlic, sesame oil and black pepper. If you have the time, refrigerate the marinade for a day on its own. Place the beef, scallions and sesame seeds into a large zip-top bag; pour the marinade on top. Compress the bag to remove excess air, then refrigerate for at least 2 hours, preferably 24 hours.

2 **TO PAN-SEAR THE MEAT:** Remove the meat from the marinade and pat dry. Preheat a large cast-iron skillet or grill pan over high heat, until smoking hot. Using a towel, rub on some vegetable oil. Working in batches, grill the marinated beef until cooked through, about 5 minutes, turning frequently until the meat begins to caramelize. Work in batches, serving the meat as it ready.

**TO GRILL THE MEAT:** Line the grill grates with foil. Heat on high until you can hold your hand 6 inches over the grate for only 2 to 3 seconds. Grill the marinated beef, uncovered, until cooked through, about 5 minutes, turning frequently until the meat begins to caramelize. Work in batches, serving the meat as it is ready.

3 Serve the beef with the rice, lettuce, perilla, kimchi and Ssamjang. To eat, make a lettuce wrap (called ssambap): take a lettuce or perilla leaf and pack on a couple spoons of rice. Layer with kimchi and some bulgogi and top with a dab of Ssamjang.

# Daeji Kalbi
## 돼지갈비

SPICY PORK SPARE RIBS

Growing up as huge fans of American-style barbecue, Matt and Deuki have rarely found a pork spare rib they didn't want to take home to mother. But unlike the typical pitmaster style—where smoke is applied in concert with indirect heat—Korean-style ribs are all about the marinade, soaking the meaty ribs in a gorgeous fruit-based sauce. This marinade, which Deuki has been making for backyard barbecues for years, needs to work its magic for at least 4 hours, but, ideally, plan ahead and just let it sit in the fridge overnight. Trust us when we say there is no better party favor than bringing over a couple freezer bags stuffed with gochujang-and-soy-marinated ribs. Throw them on the grill and the scent of Koreatown will perfume your gathering. SERVES 4

½ Asian pear, peeled and cored

1 Gala or Fuji apple, peeled and cored

½ white onion, roughly chopped

1 cup gochujang

1 tablespoon black pepper

2 tablespoons mirin

¼ cup soy sauce

¼ cup Korean rice or corn syrup

4 garlic cloves, minced

¼ cup finely ground gochugaru

2 tablespoons sugar

2 full racks baby back ribs (5 to 7 pounds total), silver skin removed

Sesame seeds, for garnish

1 Combine all ingredients except ribs and sesame seeds in a food processor or blender and process until smooth. It's best to prepare this marinade a day ahead and allow it to refrigerate, overnight, to allow the flavors to mingle.

2 Slice through the rib racks, separating the individual ribs. Combine them with the marinade in a large zip-top bag or bowl and massage for 30 seconds, until the ribs are fully coated. Allow them to marinate in the refrigerator for a minimum of 4 hours and up to 24 hours.

3 **TO GRILL:** Heat a charcoal or gas grill on medium; placing your hand 6 inches from the grate, you should be able to withstand the heat for just about 5 seconds. Remove the meat from the marinade, shaking off any excess. Grill the ribs until well-browned and cooked through, about 15 to 20 minutes, flipping frequently.

**TO ROAST:** Alternatively, preheat your oven to 350°F. Pat the ribs dry and place on a baking tray set on the top rack. Roast for 45 minutes, until the meat is tender and cooked through.

4 Remove the meat from grill or oven and allow the meat to rest for 5 minutes. Garnish with sesame seeds.

1 small white onion, pureed in a blender or food processor

¼ cup gochujang

2 tablespoons gochugaru

2 tablespoons honey powder or sugar

2 tablespoons mirin

3 garlic cloves, minced

½-inch knob of ginger, minced

1 tablespoon light soy sauce

1 tablespoon water

1 pound pork belly, sliced ⅛ inch thick

Vegetable oil, as needed

1 scallion, thinly sliced, for garnish

2 teaspoons toasted sesame seeds, for garnish

# Jeyuk Bokkeum
## 제육볶음
### STIR-FRIED PORK BELLY

*Bokkeum* is the general term given to dishes that are stir-fried over high heat, incorporating a spicy sauce to manipulate "lesser" proteins. Many classic bokkeums include seafood like octopus, mackerel and dried anchovies, but the most popular is pork belly (though you can easily substitute shoulder). This marinade has a nice balance of sweetness and spice that is brought to life when the rich pork is cooked over a high heat.

As a rule of thumb with any cooking, you do not want to mask the quality of pricey proteins by using too much seasoning or sauce. Let that thirty-day aged rib eye speak for itself! In Korea, beef is the most prized delicacy of all. So with barbecue beef, particularly kalbi (short ribs), a sparingly simple soy-based marinade is applied before the grilling begins. But pork is a totally different story: many Koreans find the smell of it to be strong, which is why Jeyuk Bokkeum is cooked in such a powerful sauce. SERVES 2 TO 4

1  Make the marinade: In a large bowl, stir together the onion, gochujang, gochugaru, honey powder, mirin, garlic, ginger, soy sauce and 1 tablespoon water. Add the pork belly, stirring to coat, and refrigerate for at least 2 hours or overnight.

2  Remove pork from the refrigerator and let sit at room temperature for 30 minutes before cooking. Heat 1 tablespoon of oil in a cast-iron skillet set over high heat until it is lightly smoking. Add the marinated pork belly, as many slices as will fit in one layer, and 2 tablespoons of the marinade. Cook, turning frequently, until caramelized, about 5 to 6 minutes. Pour out the fat, rinse or wipe the pan clean and repeat with remaining pork belly, if needed.

3  Garnish the meat with the scallion and sesame seeds and serve. Eat with a lot of rice and wrap in lettuce or perilla leaves if you are in that mood.

# ATLANTA
## HEIRLOOM MARKET BBQ

Atlanta's best barbecue restaurant is also one of the city's most hidden. Wedged between rumbling Interstate 285 and the Chattahoochee River, and sharing a parking lot with a dusty-shelved mini market well stocked with pork rinds and Mountain Dew, Heirloom Market BBQ has amassed a following not unlike San Francisco's Swan Oyster Depot or Brooklyn's Di Fara Pizza; that is, guests aren't afraid to wait in lines, sometimes longer than an hour. It's an eternity in a land where barbecue is plentiful. But Heirloom Market BBQ doesn't sell traditional barbecue, not by a long shot. In fact, it's the birthplace of modern Korean American barbecue.

---

Jiyeon Lee and Cody Taylor met while working at an upscale global bistro, Repast, before opening Heirloom Market in late 2010. Just two months later, the city's top restaurant critic, John Kessler, wrote about how the couple had "turned Atlanta barbecue on its nose." And just like that, a former Korean pop star turned chef and a self-proclaimed hillbilly from Texas pioneered Korean American barbecue.

Considering the cultures' very different ideas of barbecue, it wasn't an obvious marriage. Korean barbecue, of course, is very akin to grilling: meat meets hot iron, cooks in minutes. And, since the age of fifteen, Taylor has been doing classic American 'cue—cooking large cuts of meat, low and slow, over smoldering oak and hickory coals for a wallop of smoky flavor.

But Taylor found a partner to unite American-style barbecue with Korean flavors in his wife, Jiyeon. After spending time with family in Seoul, they bootstrapped, invested in two smokers and opened Heirloom Market BBQ in a former liquor store. There would be traditional beef brisket, a tip to Taylor's longhorn lineage, and crowd-pleasing St. Louis ribs. But Korean flavors pop up all over the place.

There's pork loin rubbed with gochujang and brisket injected with miso before they spend time in the Oyler 700 smoker. Green-tomato and okra kimchis take the place of the traditional sides (though you will always find some moist and springy corn bread). There's a kitchen sauce made with garlic, ginger, sugar, sesame oil and a Korean version of Sprite. They've played with braising the brisket in the ox-bone soup seolleongtang before smoking. There's rumor of cold-smoked swordfish belly wrapped in lettuce making an appearance.

All this just 12 miles north of downtown Atlanta in Cobb County, where the Braves plan to build a stadium in 2017, a short distance from the couple's barbecue shop. They might just be debating a bigger parking lot.

**2 tablespoons gochujang**

**1 tablespoon finely ground gochugaru**

**2 garlic cloves, minced**

**2 tablespoons sugar**

**2 tablespoons Korean rice or corn syrup**

**¼ cup soy sauce**

**2 tablespoons mirin**

**1 tablespoon sesame oil**

**1 teaspoon black pepper**

FOR THE SQUID

**2 whole large squids (1 to 1½ pounds each), cleaned**

**1 tablespoon toasted sesame seeds**

**2 scallions, thinly sliced**

# Ojinguh Gui
## 오징어구이
### BROILED WHOLE SQUID

Grilled and roasted squid (and cuttlefish) is sold by street vendors throughout Korea. Roasting whole squid might not be your typical kitchen move, but this recipe is easier than roasting a chicken, and so distinctly Korean with the union of gochujang (funk), gochugaru (heat), mirin (sweetness), soy sauce (umami!) and the tender meatiness of squid. We love this spicy marinade because it caramelizes really nicely under high heat. For this, buy your squid whole, as opposed to presliced. It will likely be fresher, and cooking it whole allows for a nice caramelization without overcooking. You should ask your fishmonger for whole large squid, cleaned with the legs reserved. SERVES 4 TO 6

1 **PREPARE THE MARINADE:** In a large bowl, combine all the marinade ingredients and whisk together until fully combined.

2 **PREPARE THE SQUID:** Cut each squid's body in ¼-inch intervals, cutting through the top of the body but not slicing all the way through to make rings. Add the bodies and the legs to the marinade, making sure the marinade coats the bodies thoroughly inside and out. Allow the squid to marinate for at least 1 hour in the refrigerator, though overnight is best.

3 Preheat the oven to 500°F.

4 Take the squid out of the marinade and remove as much of the marinade from the squid as you can. Drop the squid into an oven-safe pan, place it on the middle baking rack and roast for 6 to 8 minutes. The squid is done when the flesh becomes opaque and is firm to the touch. Slice fully through and serve with sesame seeds and scallions sprinkled on top.

¼ cup sea salt

4 whole mackerel (about ½ pound each), cleaned and butterflied

1 tablespoon vegetable oil

2 lemons, cut in half, for squeezing

# Godeungeo Gui
## 고등어구이
### QUICK-CURED BROILED MACKEREL

Mackerel is the perfect fish to enjoy simply—broiled or grilled over charcoal, with a burst of lemon—or with a bunch of kimchis and muchims and rice. Mackerel is a luxuriously oily fish with a firm flesh and unique flavor. Is it fishy? Well, sure, kinda. But fishy undersells the complexity here. There are notes of brine from a quick salt cure and a satisfying level of smokiness from a little char. And we just can't get enough of it. It's a reminder that South Korea has 3,000 miles of coastline and of the important role seafood plays in the culture.

When buying mackerel it's always good to find smaller ones, about ½ pound each—these are sweeter—and have your fishmonger clean and butterfly them for you, leaving the heads on. Serve them with a bowl of Doenjang Jjigae (page 170) and you will transport to a dockside restaurant in Busan. **SERVES 2 TO 4**

1 Salt each fish with a good amount of sea salt, about 1 tablespoon for each fish. Refrigerate for 1 hour.

2 At least 40 minutes before cooking, preheat the broiler to 500°F; 20 minutes before cooking, place a large cast-iron skillet on the top rack to preheat.

3 Remove the fish from the refrigerator and rinse under cold water to remove excess salt. Pat very dry with paper towels.

4 Pull the hot skillet out of the oven and add the oil. Place the fish in the skillet, skin side down. Broil for 3 to 4 minutes, or until the skin is nicely browned. Keep your eye on it. Remove from the oven and serve immediately with cut lemons.

# Q&A

## WHY TWO-YEAR-OLDS NEED TO EAT KALBI

Jason Ough is Matt's Korean best friend (KBF) and, with his wife, Jennie, has raised quite possibly the cutest little girl in the Bay Area, which they call home. Matt and Jason were texting about the terribleness of the New York Knicks one day, when Jason slipped in a photo of his daughter Aerim eating kalbi off the bone. Whoa! It got Matt thinking that he needed to find out from Jason about what it's like raising a very young child on Korean food.

---

**So, you just got your two-year-old daughter to eat kalbi off the bone!** *How proud are you?*

We're pretty proud. She's got all of her teeth in now—finally—so she's able to really get in there and grind the meat down. We gave her one with the bone cut off, and she had a meltdown and demanded the full piece with the bone in. So we gave it to her. And she went to town on it.

**Why is it important to cook Korean food for your daughter?**

She needs to know her heritage and where she comes from. Or at least where her grandparents come from. We want her to know that it's important—the entire ceremony of preparing, serving and eating it.

I grew up in Wisconsin. I didn't have a Korean community around me, so I never had that all-encompassing, 360-degree cultural experience. But I still had my mom, and she cooked us Korean food almost every single day. We'd drive to Chicago's Koreatown once a month to stock up and we'd keep it all in an old fridge on our back porch. It held the kimchi and other foods that were too stinky to keep alongside our "white" foods, like 2 percent milk and Wonder bread. I even bought a six-pack mini-fridge in medical school and used that as a kimchi fridge in my apartment.

So that was largely the basis of my Korean identity while growing up: our food. That's why it's so important to me, and to my wife as well. And since we want to make sure that Aerim will embrace Korean food and culture, we make it a point to get her to try as much of it as possible, teaching her the proper names and everything. And we will always have a kimchi fridge.

**But she's not really feeling kimchi yet?**

Not yet. We'll get there. We've tried, but she just cries when she tastes anything spicy. She can barely handle the mild pico de gallo from the burrito shop down the street, so it may take some trying to work up to true Korean-caliber kimchi. But she will get there. She's Korean, she has to eat kimchi. It's in her blood. It's her destiny.

# Drinking Food: Pojangmacha

안주

I n Korean culture, eating food and drinking alcohol go so hand in hand that it's often hard to separate the two. But for Koreans, drinking goes beyond partying. Drinking symbolizes respect for elders. Drinking brings people together for nearly every occasion in life—holidays, achievement, failure, the end of the workday. If you visit Koreatown in the evening, you will find packs of Korean men and women—many times sticking with their own gender—sitting at tables lined with amber- and green-shaded bottles, an unwind that will always include plates and plates of food. In this chapter we cover some of our favorite dishes that are commonly served with the near-ritualistic consumption of alcohol.

The chapter title—Pojangmacha—refers to a place Koreans visit to specifically drink and eat, and has been adapted within the Koreatowns around America.

Pojangmacha is one of the most fun Korean words to say—PO-jang-ma-CHA. The term literally means "covered wagon," and in Seoul the restaurants are modest affairs—colorful tented places lining the streets by the dozen, with stubby plastic stools and Styrofoam dinnerware. In America the restaurants, often called the abbreviated "pocha," have come indoors, but they offer a similar mix of dishes, known as anju, that are best eaten with alcohol. This includes chicken feet sauced with liquid fire (buldak bal) and soups meant to be spooned in the wee-hours (haejangguk) to prevent the inevitable hangover. While visiting L.A., one of our must-visit pochas is Dwit Gol Mok. It's a hole-in-the-wall, divey kind of place, with graffiti-tagged walls and a crowd that likes its soju early and often. *Mad Men* star Christina Hendricks, a Koreatown resident, has been known to visit. As you will find in this chapter, Koreans have drinking food nailed. 끝

# Ddangkong, Fritos, Jwipo
## 땅콩, 프리토스, 쥐포
### PEANUTS, FRITOS AND TOASTED FISH JERKY

Throughout Korea, jwipo, thin sheets of dried filefish, are sold as a popular street snack. The seasoned sheets—which you can think of as fish jerky—are toasted under an open flame to bring out their aroma, then sheared into strips. In America, they're often served as part of a snack plate at pocha-style restaurants, sometimes accompanied with dried squid and peanuts for maximum drinking maximization. One of our favorite versions of this was at a cool little buldak (fire chicken) restaurant in Chicago called Dancen, which inspired this dish, the essence of Korean food in America: dried fish, salty roasted peanuts and even saltier Fritos, with a gochujang mayo that you will basically want to dip everything in. **SERVES 4 TO 6 AS A SNACK**

1  In a small bowl, combine the mayonnaise and gochujang and mix well.

2  Heat a dry sauté pan on medium-high and toast the filefish sheets until they are warmed and slightly toasted, about 2 minutes on each side. It should smell wonderful. Remove the fish from the pan.

3  Using a knife or clean kitchen shears, cut the fish into bite-sized pieces. Place on a large serving platter with the peanuts and Fritos and serve with the gochujang mayo, which you might want to keep on hand for a future sandwich adventure.

¼ cup mayonnaise (Hellmann's or Best Foods are our picks)

1 tablespoon gochujang

6 ounces dried filefish (around 3 to 4 large sheets)

2 cups salted dry-roasted peanuts

2 cups Fritos

Salt to taste

2 bunches somen noodles

2 14-ounce cans of whelks, drained but reserving 1 tablespoon of liquid

1 English cucumber, peeled, seeded and thinly sliced

½ cup thinly sliced scallions, white parts only

1 long Korean red chile pepper, thinly sliced

1 Anaheim chile pepper, thinly sliced

½ cup thinly sliced onions

¼ cup thinly sliced carrots

½ cup julienned peeled Asian pear

4 perilla leaves, sliced

FOR THE DRESSING

3 tablespoons gochugaru

1 tablespoon gochujang

1 tablespoon reserved whelk juice

¼ cup apple or rice vinegar

2 tablespoons soy sauce

2 tablespoons sugar

1 garlic clove, minced

1 teaspoon sesame seeds

1 teaspoon sesame oil

# Golbaengi Muchim
## 골뱅이무침
### SPICY WHELK SALAD

This zippy salad, typically served cold, is both spicy and sweet and sometimes served as a banchan. People go crazy for the dish, and it's all thanks to the whelk, a cousin of the conch that tastes like a mild and pleasantly chewy clam. In America the whelk is most commonly found in scungilli, an Italian-American dish. Fresh whelk may be difficult to find, so many home cooks use the canned variety that can be found in most Asian supermarkets. This dish can also be made with more common types of canned seafood like mussels, clams or shrimp. SERVES 4

1 Boil a medium pot of well-salted water to a boil over high heat. Add the noodles and fully cook them according to the instructions on the label. While they are cooking, fill a bowl with ice-cold water. When the noodles are cooked, drain, shock them in ice water and drain well.

2 In a large bowl, combine the whelks (large pieces may be cut in half), English cucumber, scallions, chile peppers, onions, carrots, Asian pear and perilla leaves.

3 In a small bowl, combine all dressing ingredients, then combine with the salad. Serve with the noodles alongside.

# EMO:
## THE KOREAN RESTAURANT'S GATEKEEPER

The Korean word *emo* literally translates to "auntie." But the term has long taken on multiple meanings—mostly positive (it can be articulated as a term of respect), although it is sometimes used sarcastically to refer to "pushy" or strong-willed women. Many Korean restaurants around America are run by dutiful emos—hardworking gatekeepers who greet you with a warm *annyeonghaseyo!* ("hello") when you arrive, swipe your credit card at the end of your meal and generally keep the trains running in the controlled chaos of a high-volume restaurant. They will also give you sticks of fruity gum for your garlic breath. They are the Phil Jackson of the Korean restaurant, drawing up the plays and maintaining a Zen-like calm during the weekend rush.

ABOVE LEFT Park's Barbeque (Los Angeles, California) ABOVE RIGHT Baek Hwa Jung (Los Angeles, California) OPPOSITE TOP Dan Sung Sa (Duluth, Georgia) OPPOSITE BOTTOM LEFT So Moon Nan Jip (Palisades Park, New Jersey) BOTTOM OPPOSITE CENTER Soban (Los Angeles, California) OPPOSITE BOTTOM RIGHT Masil House (Fort Lee, New Jersey)

¼ cup soy sauce

2 scallions, thinly sliced

2 Korean red chile peppers, seeded and minced

2 tablespoons sugar

2 tablespoons honey or corn syrup

2 tablespoons vegetable oil

1 cup salted peanuts

4 garlic cloves, minced

1 cup dried baby anchovies

2 tablespoons toasted sesame seeds, for garnish

# Myeolchi Ddangkong Gwaja
## 멸치와땅콩과자
### ANCHOVY AND PEANUT BAR SNACK

When we first came up with this recipe we honestly could not stop stuffing our faces with it. Dried fish is the quintessential Korean bar snack, served at pojangmachas and karaoke halls to inspire more drinking. In America, peanuts serve the same purpose. We bring the two together in this addictively salty, umami-packed snack. Using high heat is important, because it will quickly toast the peanuts and caramelize the sauce. But as with all high-heat cooking, be mindful of burning. You can find tiny dried anchovies at any Asian supermarket or grocery store. And here's a tip: Make this instead of guacamole for your next NFL playoff party. A few of your friends might be like "WTF bro" to start. But watch as the bowl empties before halftime. **SERVES 4 TO 6 AS A SNACK**

1 Make the sauce by mixing together the soy sauce, scallions, red chile peppers, sugar and honey in a small bowl.

2 In a large sauté pan, heat the vegetable oil over medium-high heat until it shimmers. Add the peanuts and toast, stirring, for 30 seconds. Add garlic and anchovies and sauté for another 30 seconds, until very fragrant. Add the sauce and cook for another 45 seconds to coat and form a glaze on the peanuts and anchovies. Garnish with sesame seeds and serve warm.

# Dakgangjeong

## 닭강정

### KOREATOWN FRIED CHICKEN

When it comes to the art of frying chicken, Koreans could give Southerners a run for their money. There, said it. Korean fried chicken (KFC) chains have set up shop in the Koreatowns of New York, Chicago, Atlanta and Los Angeles. KFC combines savory, spicy glazes and skin that shatters like glass. And guess what? We have the secret. Booyah!

Many have said that frying the chicken twice achieves a next-level crunch, which we aren't going to deny. But the real key is the batter. Ours uses soju, which inhibits gluten formation and keeps the batter light. If you have a little extra time, we highly recommend partially frying the chicken, then freezing it for at least 2 hours before a second fry.

We offer recipes for two classic sauces you will find at Koreatown chicken joints: spicy and soy garlic. You can also simply season with salt and pepper and dot with Frank's Red Hot, which elevates any fried chicken experience, Korean or otherwise. **SERVES 4**

**8 cups vegetable oil**

**2 pounds chicken wings or thighs**

**½ cup cornstarch**

**½ cup all-purpose flour**

**½ teaspoon baking powder**

**1 teaspoon kosher salt, plus more to taste**

**½ cup soju or vodka**

**½ cup ice-cold water**

**Soy Garlic Glaze or Hot Sauce Glaze (recipes follow)**

**¼ cup sliced scallions**

**1** Heat the vegetable oil over low heat in a heavy pot or Dutch oven with high sides until the oil registers 350°F on a frying thermometer. If you don't have a thermometer, test the heat by spooning a bit of batter into the oil. If it sizzles immediately and floats to the top, chances are you're ready. (If you're using chicken wings, while the oil heats, use a sharp knife to feel for the joints between the wings and drumettes, and cut through to separate them.)

**2** In a medium bowl, whisk together the cornstarch, all-purpose flour, baking powder, 1 teaspoon salt, soju and cold water. Dip chicken parts in batter until evenly coated, shaking off excess batter, and place on a platter or tray.

**3** Set up a tray or platter lined with paper towels. Raise the heat to medium-high and maintain the oil at 350°F. Carefully lower the chicken into the oil, as many pieces as will fit comfortably, and fry for 8 to 10 minutes, until golden brown and cooked through. With a heatproof slotted spoon, remove the chicken pieces and drain them on the paper-towel-lined tray. Immediately season with salt. While still hot, toss the chicken in a large bowl with just enough glaze to coat. Garnish with scallions and serve immediately.

**A RECOMMENDATION**: Instead of frying for the full 8 to 10 minutes, fry just until the skin reaches a light blonde, 4 to 5 minutes. Cool on a paper-towel-lined tray until room temperature and freeze for at least 2 hours and up to overnight. When you are ready to serve, heat the frying oil to 375°F and drop the cold, partially fried chicken in for 4 to 5 minutes, until deep golden brown and cooked through. Immediately season with salt, toss with glaze, and garnish with scallions. Adding the frozen, partially cooked chicken to hot oil is the key to achieving the ideal crust. In nerdier terms, the water particles in the crust freeze, and as a result the ice shards break open the starch cells, creating more surface area to crisp. Shouts to Francis Lam for that info.

## SOY GARLIC GLAZE

MAKES ENOUGH FOR 1 BATCH OF FRIED CHICKEN

**¼ cup Korean rice or corn syrup**

**¼ cup soy sauce**

**2 garlic cloves, minced**

**1 tablespoon mirin**

**1 tablespoon sesame oil**

Combine syrup, soy sauce, garlic and mirin in a small saucepan and bring to a boil over high heat. Boil for 1 minute. Allow to cool to room temperature and stir in sesame oil. Hold until ready to use.

## HOT SAUCE GLAZE

MAKES ENOUGH FOR 1 BATCH OF FRIED CHICKEN

**½ cup gochujang**

**5 tablespoons Frank's Red Hot**

Combine gochujang and hot sauce in a small bowl and whisk together until smooth. Hold until ready to use.

**1 pound chicken feet**

**4 tablespoons salt**

**2-inch knob of ginger, grated**

**6 whole garlic cloves**

**½ cup soju or vodka**

**1 quart vegetable oil**

**¼ cup cornstarch**

**4 scallions, finely sliced, for garnish**

**Sesame seeds, for garnish**

FOR THE SAUCE

**2 tablespoons gochujang**

**¼ cup finely ground gochugaru**

**3 tablespoons Korean rice or corn syrup**

**1 tablespoon sugar**

**½ cup soy sauce**

**8 garlic cloves, minced**

**½ tablespoon black pepper**

**½-inch knob of ginger, grated**

**2 tablespoons vegetable oil**

**1 Chungyang red chile pepper (or serrano), thinly sliced**

**½ cup chicken stock**

# Buldak Bal
## 불닭발
### FIRE CHICKEN FEET

You are going to have to go with us a bit on this one. The wonderful leftover parts of chicken are a big part of Asian cooking, which is why you will find piles and piles of hearts, livers and feet in the butcher's case in your local Koreatown. Many Koreans absolutely love spicy and gelatinous chicken feet with their drinks: it's a quintessential anju. We do realize nibbling the skin off nubby appendages is not for everybody, which is why we've created a recipe that elevates the texture while staying true to tradition. And if you're really not into feet, you can toss any grilled chicken meat with the sauce. (See photo.)

Instead of simply boiling, we like to lightly fry the feet before tossing in a peppery gochujang–soy sauce. While this dish, like Prince's *20Ten*, is in the "for fans only" zone, the sauce really hits a lot of the notes everybody loves: spice, sweetness, soy sauce. As the name "fire chicken" implies, the gochujang you buy for this should be as spicy as you can stand. And for chiles, look for the tiny Chungyang red pepper, which is one of the hottest found in Korea, similar to the serrano. That should get the fire started. SERVES 4

1 Usually when you buy chicken feet, they are in need of a pedicure. Remove the claws by cutting off the tips with kitchen shears. Toss with 2 tablespoons of salt and let sit for 10 minutes.

2 In a large pot, combine 8 cups water, 2 tablespoons salt, ginger, whole garlic and soju and bring to a boil over high heat. Add the chicken feet and blanch at a full boil for 20 minutes.

3 To make the sauce, in a small bowl combine the gochujang, gochugaru, rice syrup, sugar, soy sauce, 6 cloves minced garlic, black pepper and grated ginger. Set aside.

4 Heat 2 tablespoons of oil in a medium saucepan on medium-high. When hot, add 2 cloves minced garlic. When fragrant, add most of the chiles, chicken stock and gochujang mixture. Cook until the mixture coats the back of a spoon. Set aside in a large bowl; you will be tossing the chicken feet around, so there should be plenty of room.

**5** In a large, high-sided saucepan with a few inches of clearance, heat 1 quart oil over medium heat to 350°F on a frying thermometer. Fill a large bowl with ice water; remove chicken feet from boiling pot and shock them in the ice water. Drain, shake excess water off and pat the feet very dry with paper towels. In a large bowl, toss the feet in cornstarch to lightly coat. When the oil is ready, raise the heat to medium-high and deep-fry the feet for 4 minutes, until golden brown. Meanwhile, line a large bowl with paper towels.

**6** Remove chicken feet from oil and drain in paper-towel-lined bowl. Immediately drop the chicken feet into the large bowl with sauce, tossing to coat. Garnish with remaining sliced chiles, scallions and sesame seeds. Serve immediately with a cold bottle of soju.

# Tongdak
## 통닭

### WHOLE ROASTED CHICKEN

When writing an "ethnic fusion" roasted chicken recipe, some recipe writers are inclined to go all over-the-top Guy Fieri with a gochujang lacquer and a wasabi–mashed potato side dish bad boy. We take a slightly different approach. This is actually a classic dish served in Koreatowns at hofs—their interpretation of German-style beer halls. The bird, preferably organic, is stuffed with a distinctly Korean trio of whole garlic cloves, ginger and scallions. Once roasted in a cast-iron skillet, pair the tender meat with soy sauce–pickled vegetables, water radish kimchi and pretty much anything fermented in our Banchan chapter (page 34). We've also included a really simple, spicy dipping sauce. It's no Donkey Sauce, but we think our Guy would approve. **SERVES 2 TO 4**

**1** Preheat the oven to 450°F and heat a large cast-iron skillet in it for 30 minutes.

**2** Meanwhile, rinse the chicken under cold water and pat very dry, inside and out, with paper towels. Season the inside of the chicken's cavity with salt and stuff it with the garlic, ginger and scallions. Truss the chicken by tying the ends of the legs together with butcher's twine.

**3** Rub the chicken all over with 2 tablespoons of vegetable oil and season generously all over with salt and pepper. Remove the cast-iron skillet from the oven (careful, it's really hot!) and swirl in 1 tablespoon of oil; it will probably start smoking. Place the chicken, breast side up, in the cast-iron skillet and place it in the oven.

**4** Roast the chicken for 40 to 50 minutes, until the juices run clear when you poke the thigh with a sharp knife. While the bird is roasting, combine the gochujang and Frank's Red Hot in a small bowl. (That's your dipping sauce. We took this idea from Dale Talde. Dale knows what is up.) When the chicken is cooked, remove it from the pan and rest on a cutting board for 10 minutes. Serve with Quick Soy Sauce Pickles and Water Radish Kimchi.

1 organic chicken (about 3 pounds)

Kosher salt to taste

6 whole garlic cloves

2-inch knob of ginger, roughly chopped

2 scallions

3 tablespoons vegetable oil

1 teaspoon freshly cracked black pepper

¼ cup gochujang

¼ cup Frank's Red Hot

1 cup assorted Quick Soy Sauce Pickles (page 49), for serving

1 cup Water Radish Kimchi (page 45), for serving

**2 tablespoons gochujang**

**2 tablespoons gochugaru**

**1 tablespoon sugar**

**2 tablespoons corn syrup**

**¼ cup mirin**

**2 tablespoons sesame oil**

**3 cups finely shredded dried squid**

**Black sesame seeds, for garnish**

# Ojingeochae Muchim

## 오징어채무침

### SPICY-SWEET SHREDDED SQUID

Unlike the Western food world, where soft and tender is coveted, Koreans enjoy the art of the chew. Chewy rice cakes. Chewy fish cakes. And chewy dried squid, essentially jerky, is the star of this snack. Dried squid can be an acquired taste for some, especially in its roughest, aquarium-est form. But there's also some serious sweet-salty magic going on with dried squid. Mix it with gochujang, mirin, sesame oil and sugar and it becomes something entirely new—an addictive snack, often served as anju (to be paired with soju and beer), and its jerky-like texture becomes more enjoyable with each bite. Make sure the dried squid you are using is finely shredded. Eat it straight up or with a bowl of rice for a quick and tasty snack. SERVES 4 TO 6 AS A SNACK

1 In a small bowl, mix the gochujang, gochugaru, sugar, syrup, mirin and sesame oil until combined.

2 Heat a large sauté pan on high and add ¼ cup of water. Add the dried squid and spread it out in the pan. Cook for 3 minutes on high, or until the water is mostly evaporated.

3 Add the gochujang mixture and continue to cook until the sauce has fully incorporated with the squid, glazing it. Serve at room temperature, sprinkled with sesame, or refrigerate for up to a week.

# Jokbal
## 족발
### SOY-BRAISED PIG'S FEET

A classic anju dish, braised pig's feet is a dare-worthy (to some) fixture of the late-night pocha scene in Koreatowns across the country. Why do jokbal junkies crave it? The tender meat, soft cartilage and fat offer a unique combination of texture and flavor, which goes really well with a fifth punch-you-in-the-teeth shot of soju. But even if you're not drinking, they are pretty delicious all the same when braised in soy sauce and a fragrant combination of aromatics and spices.
SERVES 4 TO 6

1  Soak the trotters in water, in the refrigerator, for 4 hours, to remove impurities and any loose fragments. Rinse well and set aside.

2  In a large pot, bring 4 cups of water and soju to a boil. Add the trotters and boil for 30 minutes; drain.

3  Add the trotters and the remaining ingredients to a pressure cooker or large Dutch oven. If you're using a pressure cooker, braise for 30 minutes over medium-high heat; if using a Dutch oven, bring the liquid to a boil over high heat, then lower it to a gentle simmer. Cover and simmer for 2 hours over medium or medium-low heat, until the trotters are very tender.

4  Remove trotters from the braising liquid; reserve both. When cool enough to handle, carefully remove the meat from the bones and slice if desired. Place meat in a bowl and moisten with some of the braising liquid.

5  Strain some of the braising liquid and add to a wide saucepan. Bring to a boil and reduce over medium heat to thicken it to a rich, but pourable, sauce-like consistency. Place the warm trotters on a platter and serve sauce on the side.

**4 pounds pig trotters**

**½ cup soju or vodka**

**1 cup soy sauce**

**¼ cup light brown sugar**

**¼ cup Korean rice or corn syrup**

**12 garlic cloves, halved**

**4 scallions, sliced**

**1 medium onion, halved**

**2 cups peeled and large-dice daikon**

**2 tablespoons sliced ginger**

**1 tablespoon whole black peppercorns**

**1 tablespoon kosher salt**

**3 dried Korean red chile peppers**

**3 bay leaves**

**2 cinnamon sticks**

**1 pound chuck flap or rib eye, sliced thin**

**½ cup peeled, cored and thinly sliced Asian pear**

**½ cup thinly sliced Persian cucumbers**

**1 tablespoon pine nuts**

**1 egg yolk**

**Salt and pepper to taste**

FOR THE MARINADE

**2 tablespoons soy sauce**

**2 tablespoons sugar**

**1 tablespoon finely minced white onion**

**1 garlic clove, finely minced**

**1 teaspoon freshly cracked black pepper**

**2 teaspoons sesame seeds**

**1 tablespoon sesame oil**

# Yukhoe
# 육회

## SOY-MARINATED BEEF TARTARE

The first time Matt saw a plate of yukhoe—marbled, raw chopped beef topped with a just-separated egg yolk—he assumed that it was for the grill. Had he stumbled on Korea's long-forgotten version of a hamburger? But soon his Korean friends mixed in the egg and started to eat the chilled meat, and it was clear that he was in for something else. Something good. Snacking on raw beef is of course nothing new, from Ethiopian kitfo to the steak tartare you spooned during your last trip to Canal Saint-Martin. The Korean version includes a sweet-savory-pungent marinade and crisp garnishes, and it is absolutely simple to make at home. It's one of our favorites to start a meat-centric Korean barbecue feast or to pair with a bubbling jjigae. When preparing yukhoe at home, the quality of the meat, obviously, is important—you want to buy from your most-trusted butcher. And make sure to pull the meat out of the refrigerator only when you are ready to serve. The meat should be cold and firm when presented at the table—never at room temperature like you will find it in Europe. Serving yukhoe ice-cold, even with a few frozen crystals, is the true Korean way. SERVES 4

1 Slice the meat into batons about ¼ inch wide. Reserve in a bowl.

2 Place the meat in a freezer, along with an empty serving bowl, and chill until the meat is firm and just beginning to freeze, about 20 minutes. The thinner you slice the meat, the quicker it will freeze.

3 While the meat is freezing, make the marinade by combining all the ingredients in a bowl.

4 Remove the meat from the freezer right before you are going to serve and toss it in the marinade. The meat should still remain very cold, so do not over-toss.

5 Place the meat in the center of the chilled serving bowl. Garnish with the Asian pear, cucumbers, pine nuts and egg yolk. Season with salt and pepper and serve immediately, mixing the yolk into the meat at the table.

# Bossam

## 보쌈

### CRISPY PORK BELLY

Bossam is less a dish and more of an event. Traditionally, it's a large piece of pork belly served with a host of side dishes and condiments that are paired together in various combinations, wrapped in lettuce leaves and eaten. It's all very festive and communal—and it also features a plate of raw oysters, which is a pretty badass touch. David Chang (see our interview, page 88), a great chef and even better businessman, does a version with roasted pork shoulder at his New York City restaurant Momofuku Ssam Bar. (Run, don't walk.)

Our version takes some advance planning but is certainly doable for even the most novice home cook, and we've paid close attention to texture. Traditionally, the pork is boiled for hours and hours (sometimes beyond identification)—but wait, you like crispy better than mushy? Us too! After a quick boil-and-chill (ideally overnight), the pork belly gets some time under the broiler to perfect the crunchy skin. Serve with savory ssamjang, daikon kimchi and raw oysters, if you'd like. A couple of bottles of ice-cold soju will do you no wrong. SERVES 8 TO 10

1 Rinse the belly well under cold water. Using a sharp skewer or the tip of a small knife, prick the skin with tiny holes just below the surface of the skin, but be careful not to pierce into the meat. We're talking 150 to 200 pricks. We promise this effort will be worth it. (The holes let the fat render out more quickly. Oh, and it fries the skin to a crisp on its way out too.)

2 In a large Dutch oven or stockpot, combine 8 cups water, kosher salt, doenjang, instant coffee, onion, garlic, ginger and jujubes and bring to a boil over high heat. Boil for 5 minutes. Add the pork belly and adjust the heat to maintain a simmer. Simmer for 25 minutes.

3 Remove the meat from the pot, drain, and pat the skin very dry with paper towels. Put it on a plate and refrigerate, uncovered, for at least 5 hours, preferably overnight. This will dry out the skin.

4 Preheat the oven to 400°F.

(recipe continues)

3 pounds pork belly, skin on

8 cups water

¼ cup kosher salt

2 tablespoons doenjang

1 tablespoon instant ground coffee

1 medium onion, cut into large dice

6 garlic cloves

1-inch knob of ginger, cut in half

4 dried jujubes

1 teaspoon white vinegar

½ cup coarse sea salt

1 cup Dried Daikon Radish Muchim (page 53)

½ cup Ssamjang (page 115)

12 raw oysters, for serving (optional)

Salted Cabbage (recipe follows)

2 heads Bibb lettuce, leaves washed, separated and dried

**5** Poke more holes in the skin! (Seriously, the more the better.) Rub the skin with white vinegar and coat with coarse sea salt. Do not use kosher or fine sea salt or it will become too salty.

**6** Fill an oven-safe bowl with water and place it on lowest oven rack. This will create steam. Place the belly skin side up on a rack set over a sheet pan, and place that in the center of the oven. Roast for 25 minutes and remove from the oven. The skin should start to turn golden by now.

**7** Turn the heat to broil (on the low setting, if you have one) and allow it to preheat.

**8** Brush off the salt from the belly's skin. When the broiler is preheated, place the belly on the top rack and broil until the skin is very crisp and richly browned but not burnt. Keep an eye on it throughout the process. Remove the belly and allow it to rest for 5 minutes. Slice thin and serve with Dried Daikon Radish Muchim, Ssamjang, freshly shucked oysters, Salted Cabbage and lettuce for wrapping the bites.

## SALTED CABBAGE
SERVES 8 TO 10

**¼ cup salt**

**¼ cup sugar**

**1 head napa cabbage, cored and quartered**

Mix together the salt and sugar. Rub the mixture on the cut cabbage and allow it to sit for 2 hours. Once cured, shake off excess sugar and salt.

# Saengseontwikim
## 생선튀김
### FISH AND CHIPS

We like to think of Korean fried fish as KFC 2.0: like our fried chicken recipe (see page 141), the key is the batter, incorporating soju and Korean beer like Hite or OB (though Guinness works nicely as well). The batter is light as a cloud, with maximum crunch. As an extra step, dust with homemade Kimchi Salt (recipe on following page). **SERVES 2**

1 In a large heavy pot or Dutch oven that can comfortably accommodate the fish and oil with a few inches of clearance, heat the oil over medium-low heat until it reaches 375°F on a frying thermometer.

2 While the oil heats, prep the fish by patting it dry with paper towels and then, with a sharp knife, scoring the body to the bone in 1-inch intervals. Generously season the fish on both sides with salt and pepper, then dust lightly with flour. Set aside.

3 In a large bowl that will fit the whole fish, whisk together ½ cup all-purpose flour, cornstarch, baking powder and 1 teaspoon salt. When well mixed, whisk in the soju and beer just until the batter is smooth. Dip the scored snapper in the batter, making sure all the crevices are covered, and place it on a plate.

4 If necessary, increase the heat to bring the oil to 375°F and maintain the temperature. Hold the snapper by its tail and submerge it, head-first, into the oil; hold it there for 15 seconds. Then carefully release the fish and fry for 7 to 9 minutes, until it's a rich golden brown and just cooked through at the thickest part, where the body meets the neck. Line a platter with paper towels. When cooked, carefully remove the fish from the oil with tongs or large straining spoons and drain it on the paper towels. Immediately season with salt and pepper (or Kimchi Salt) to taste. Garnish with scallions.

5 Fry the sweet potatoes for 6 to 8 minutes, until browned and crisp. Line another platter with paper towels. Remove the fries with a strainer and let them drain on paper towels. Season with Kimchi Salt or salt and pepper to taste and serve.

**2 quarts canola or vegetable oil**

**1 whole red snapper (about 2 pounds), scaled and cleaned**

**Kosher salt and black pepper to taste**

**All-purpose flour for dusting, plus ½ cup**

**½ cup cornstarch**

**½ teaspoon baking powder**

**¼ cup soju or vodka**

**¾ cup Hite or OB beer (or Guinness)**

**Kimchi Salt (page 158, optional)**

**1 scallion, thinly sliced, for garnish**

**2 sweet potatoes, cut into 3 × ½-inch batons**

1½ cups dried baby shrimp

½ cup garlic powder

½ cup onion powder

1 cup coarsely ground gochugaru

1½ teaspoons ground coriander

1½ teaspoons citric acid powder

1 tablespoon ginger powder

1 cup kosher salt

# Kimchi Salt

Deuki created this recipe with the intention of capturing the essence of kimchi in a powdered form. Why? Because the essence of kimchi in a powdered form makes a pretty incredible seasoning for things like French fries, popcorn, fried fish and steamed vegetables. We like to call it the Korean Old Bay, with the union of garlic, ginger and onion with spice and the brine of the sea.

A few things to keep in mind. First, the shrimp microwave-drying step requires some patience. Make sure to work in 30-second intervals—tops! Nuking any longer might burn the shrimp, which is not a good thing. Alternatively, if you own a dehydrator, it will work great here. Second, make sure your kitchen is as well ventilated as possible because heating up dried shrimp very well could piss off your neighbors (if you live in an urban setting). Third, a Vitamix is ideal for pulverizing the dried shrimp. A less powerful blender may not create the most powdery consistency, but a coffee grinder could work here, depending on your model. Let us assure you that this is all worth it. Plus, we've written this recipe to yield a bunch so you can make a batch and have it around for a while. **MAKES ABOUT 3 CUPS**

1 Place the dried shrimp on a microwave-safe plate and cover it with paper towel. Nuke the shrimp in 30-second intervals, allowing for the shrimp to air out for 30 seconds between heatings. Continue until the shrimp has turned slightly white, around 8 to 10 intervals. Once dried, allow the shrimp to cool for 15 minutes. (Don't be tempted to zap it all in one go, which will likely burn the shrimp.)

2 Combine the garlic powder, onion powder, gochugaru, coriander, citric acid, ginger powder and dried shrimp in a high-powered blender like a Vitamix. If you don't own one, pulverize the shrimp by itself, in batches, in a coffee grinder and mix all the powders together in a large bowl.

3 Thoroughly combine the flavorings with kosher salt. The Kimchi Salt will keep in your pantry in an airtight container for several months.

# EATING KOREATOWN
## ACTOR ANDY MILONAKIS

While most people know Andy Milonakis from his cult MTV2 sketch comedy show, we've gotten to know Milonakis as a really smart food guy.

It's midnight, and we are sitting across from the actor at a 24-hour goat spot in Los Angeles. Bulrocho is slightly anonymous, if you discount the six-foot goats painted on the sign. "This is the bomb," he says of the goat hot pot bubbling at the center of the table. We pull apart pieces of the tender meat and dip them into hot mustard. The broth grabs our attention, peppery with wild sesame and mustard seeds.

"I still need to get schooled in the name of dishes, but I know what I like," he says after showing us photos of his last trip for Korean-style sashimi called hwe. "I set out to eat at Korean restaurants that were not barbecue." Milonakis represents a small but growing population of Korean food fans: non-Koreans who've been bitten by the Korean barbecue bug and are inter-

ested—sometimes religious—about branching out in the other categories. The Korean kitchen's deep bench of soups and stews is often a starting point, but the quest for discovery can lead to restaurants specializing in raw fish, dumplings and braised intestines. "I have a lot of work left to do," wrote *New York Times* restaurant critic Pete Wells in his December 2014 exploration of the "kimchi belt" in Queens.

For the comic, his quest to think outside the lettuce wrap led to discovering a world of blood sausage called soondae and "bomb jokbal." And then, there was also a night spent feasting on platters of raw, slightly rotting, fish dressed with scallions and cho-jang. "That was a bit gnarly, but I was pretty drunk," he says of his experience with hongeohoe, fermented skate that oozes ammonia through its skin.

2 heads baby napa cabbage (about 1 pound each)

3 tablespoons doenjang

2 tablespoons gochugaru

4 garlic cloves, minced

2 tablespoons soy sauce

1 tablespoon sesame oil

¾ cup bean sprouts

½ cup sliced zucchini

1 scallion, thinly sliced

1 Korean red chile pepper, thinly sliced

1 Anaheim chile pepper, thinly sliced

5 cups Beef Stock (page 197)

# Haejangguk
## 해장국
### HANGOVER STEW

After a long night of drinking, there are certain foods we retreat to that simply make us feel better. Some swear by Kraft mac and cheese (with dashes of Tabasco, obviously) or a box of Popeye's chicken and biscuits. In Korea, there is a soup made specifically for the occasion when you may have gone a little crazy with the Fernet shots. Haejangguk literally means "hangover soup" and works as a way to getting your body back to a level playing field. The broth is rich and unquestionably beefy, but not over-the-top spicy. It gets its character, though, from marinating vegetables for a few minutes with a doenjang-forward paste before just cooking them through.

The soup is typically made with chunks of oxtail meat and cubes of coagulated blood, but we've simplified things a bit here, focusing on the vegetables and beef broth. And a note to teetotalers or those smart enough to avoid a bone-crushing hangover: Haejangguk is for you too!

SERVES 4 TO 6

1 Fill a large pot with water and bring it to a boil over high heat. Fill a large bowl with ice water and set it nearby. Blanch both whole cabbages for 1 minute, then drain and drop them into the ice water to stop the cooking. Drain and cut each into 2-inch pieces.

2 In a large bowl, combine the doenjang, gochugaru, garlic, soy sauce and sesame oil. Add the blanched cabbage, bean sprouts, zucchini, scallion and chile peppers and mix well. Allow to marinate at room temperature for 15 minutes.

3 Transfer the contents of the mixing bowl back to the emptied blanching pot and add the stock. Bring to a boil over high heat, then lower to a simmer for 10 minutes. Serve.

# Jogaetang
## 조개탕
### SPICY CLAM SOUP

It's late. You need something to make you feel right again, but you don't want that volleyball-in-your-gut feeling the next morning. For many Koreans, the answer is jogaetang—a light, satisfying clam soup that is often served at pojangmachas on a portable butane burner and paired with beer and soju. In a good pot of jogaetang, the clear broth evokes the essence of the sea, so it's a little briny, but not in an overpowering way. Heat from the jalapeños can be adjusted to your liking, but it shouldn't overpower the dish either. The name of the game is balance and resetting the palate for the next round of drinks and snacks. SERVES 4

2 pounds littleneck clams, scrubbed

3 cups water

1 4 × 4-inch square of kombu

1 garlic clove, sliced

1 jalapeño pepper, sliced, with seeds

1 Korean or Anaheim chile pepper, sliced

Sea salt, to taste

1 scallion, cut into 2-inch pieces, for garnish (optional)

1  Soak clams in cold water for 1 hour. This will rid them of sand and sediment. Lift the clams from the water, leaving the grit behind.

2  In a large saucepan, bring 3 cups of water and the kombu to a boil over high heat. Boil for 3 minutes and remove the kombu.

3  Add clams, garlic, jalapeño and Korean chile pepper and boil for 4 minutes, or until the clam shells open. If there are stubborn closed clams, remove the opened clams to a bowl and continue to cook the unopened clams for a few more minutes. If they still don't open, discard them. Add salt to taste. Divide the soup in bowls with the clams, garnish with scallions and serve immediately.

2 cups fresh or thawed frozen fish cakes

4 cups Anchovy Stock (page 195)

1 cup ¼-inch slices of daikon radish

1 garlic clove, minced

2 tablespoons soy sauce

1 Korean red chile pepper, thinly sliced, for garnish

2 scallions, thinly sliced, for garnish

1 small bunch of chrysanthemum greens, for garnish

# Eomuktang
## 어묵탕
### FISH CAKE SOUP

Fish cake soup might not roll off the tongue like spaghetti carbonara, but many Koreans crave this light, savory soup beyond belief—it's briny, spicy and salty in a way that pairs wonderfully with an ice-cold bottle of soju. That is why this dish is always found on pochjangmacha menus and ordered until dawn. The unique spongy texture and deeply satisfying flavor of the fish cakes is a seriously winning combination.

You can find fish cakes of various sizes (typically made with hake or whiting) sold frozen at all Asian grocery stores. Make sure to leave them out to thaw an hour before cooking. Some of the best Korean dishes are the ones that are the simplest to prepare, and this is a classic example.
SERVES 2

1  Cut the fish cakes into 2 × 2-inch squares, or any uniform shape. Thread them onto 2 bamboo skewers.

2  Bring the Anchovy Stock, fish cake skewers, daikon, garlic and soy sauce to a boil in a small pot over high heat. Lower the heat and simmer for about 10 minutes, or until the flavors come together. Garnish with peppers, scallions and chrysanthemum greens, which will wilt into the soup. Serve immediately.

# Soups, Stews & Braises

---

# 국 찌개 & 찜

There's a faded letter tacked to the corkboard wall at New York City's Han Bat, written in Korean for all the Korean-speaking world to see when entering the 35th Street artifact. "You won't find better cooking in Korea," jokes the note's author about the superior country-style soups and stews at this sometimes forgotten little treasure, tucked between the better-known Cho Dang Gol and Madangsui. Though it's open 24 hours a day, serving a breakfast menu of yukgaejang (spicy beef soup) and seolleongtang (a milky ox-bone broth seasoned with green onions and powdery salt), you'll find it most crowded at night—a mix of urbanite Koreans and in-the-know non-Koreans looking for steaming bowls of comfort. Korean tourists come with suitcases, fueling up on makgeolli and gamjatang (a peppery pork neck, wild sesame and potato soup) before their late-night flights to Incheon. Grilled meat plays second fiddle to the home-style soups and stews executed with the exacting hand of a Korean grandmother.

Korea is a *very* cold place in the wintertime. Like Minnesota and Stockholm cold, with snow blanketing much of the country for months at a time. It's natural soup weather—which may be why Koreans are kings of the one-pot dinner.

Kongbiji jjigae is one of these dishes. Unlike the more common soondubu jjigae (chunks of silky tofu floating in a fiery broth), this dish is made from tofu blended to a porridge-like consistency. It's nutty and offered with or without chunks of pork sausage. It's a greatly satisfying dish hardly known outside of Korean circles—served literally boiling, forcing diners to wait or suffer the palate-scalding consequences. But most Koreans (and card-carrying Korean food fans) have their blow-on-the-spoon technique down, because these intensely hot soups and stews (in both temperature and spice) are vital to understanding Korean cuisine.

In this chapter we cover a lot of the classics—the soups and stews of Korea could be their own anchovy stock–splattered tome—while lighter broths and some delicious chicken-based dishes expand the conversation. And, of course, we have our recipe for gamjatang, no suitcase required. 끝

# Kimchi Jjigae
## 김치찌개
### KIMCHI STEW

Kimchi jjigae is the great utility dish of Korean cooking, a quick stew full of the flavors of napa cabbage kimchi (and juice), doenjang, gochujang and gochugaru. It's often placed at the center of the table for a simple dinner or alongside a barbecue feast. Like chicken soup, there are many ways to cook it right. We think the best way is to use extra-aged kimchi, which establishes the pleasant sourness the dish is famous for. If you cannot find older kimchi (called mukgeunji—you can ask for it at the Korean grocery store), take your jar of new kimchi and leave it out at room temperature for a day or two. The best way to enjoy this Korean hot pot is to pack a long-handled spoon with a little rice and dip into the bubbling pot. Eat. Smile. Repeat. SERVES 2 TO 4

1 In a large saucepan, combine kimchi, kimchi juice, pork, doenjang, gochujang, gochugaru, sugar and onion. Place over high heat and cook for 5 minutes, stirring occasionally.

2 When the stew is a dark red and has a pungent roasted-kimchi aroma, add Pork Stock and tofu and bring to a boil. Lower the heat and simmer for 15 minutes, until the flavors have married.

3 Garnish with scallions and serve in the pot at the table, ideally while still boiling. Be careful! Eat with rice.

2 cups roughly chopped long-fermented cabbage kimchi

½ cup kimchi juice

¼ pound pork belly or leg, cut into strips

1 tablespoon doenjang

1 tablespoon gochujang

2 teaspoons gochugaru

1 tablespoon sugar

1 small onion, sliced thin

4 cups Pork Stock (page 196)

7 ounces silken tofu, cut into small cubes

1 scallion, sliced thin, for garnish

¼ cup doenjang

2 garlic cloves, minced

1 teaspoon gochugaru

¼ pound flavorful cut of beef, such as short ribs, chuck, or skirt steak, diced

¼ cup half-moon slices of Korean squash or zucchini

¼ cup diced onions

1 scallion, cut into 1-inch lengths

8 ounces soft tofu, cut into small cubes

½ Korean or Anaheim chile, sliced thin, with seeds

¼ pound littleneck clams, scrubbed and soaked in water for 30 minutes (optional)

3 cups Beef Stock (page 197)

# Doenjang Jjigae
## 된장 찌개
### BEAN PASTE STEW

Fermented bean paste, doenjang, is a fundamental ingredient in Korean cooking and is used in what is arguably Korea's most-popular stew, doenjang jjigae—a staple of the Korean home kitchen and served at all hours of the day, from breakfast to late-night. Doenjang's earthiness, saltiness and crazy depth of flavor will make you crave a bowl on your drive home from work or in the middle of yoga class. The need for doenjang jjigae will attack you out of the blue. Just a little fair warning before making your first bowl.

Our recipe is as simple, and traditional, as it comes, with tofu, squash and the heat of Korean chile working in concert with clams and the funky paste. And one more thing about doenjang: Many people describe it as being just like Japanese miso, which is simply not true. "You can call it miso just like you call a girl a ho: that is, you can't," writes chef Roy Choi in his book *L.A. Son.* It's a matter of Korean pride, for sure, and it's tough to really describe the difference between the two without going into a large discussion, perhaps politically motivated, that should probably be left out of a recipe headnote. But please, do not substitute miso for doenjang in this recipe. Doenjang is available at most Asian supermarkets and easy to spot. It's in the brown tub. SERVES 2 TO 4

1 Mix the doenjang, garlic and gochugaru into a paste in a medium saucepan. Add beef, squash, onions, scallion, tofu, chile and clams (if using).

2 Stir the Beef Stock into the saucepan and bring it to a boil over high heat. Lower the heat, cover and simmer for 20 minutes to marry the flavors. Serve with rice.

# Soondubu Jjigae
## 순두부 찌개
### SOFT TOFU STEW

The famous Korean silken tofu soup—called soondubu (*dubu* is the word for "tofu" in Korean)—is a fan favorite, and many Koreatown restaurants exist solely to sell the stuff. It's healing, warming and incredibly satisfying from the first autumn chill to the darkest winter afternoon. When we eat soondubu, we like each bite to include a smooth chunk of tofu, which is why we call for barely cutting the block of tofu. With your spoon, scoop a little tofu, grab a little broth, blow and eat. SERVES 2 TO 4

1 Combine garlic, gochugaru, mirin, black pepper, soy sauce and salt in a bowl and whisk together.

2 In a medium saucepan, combine the gochugaru mixture, tofu, mushrooms, onion and Anchovy Stock.

3 Bring to a boil over high heat, then lower the heat and simmer for 15 minutes so the flavors can marry. Serve immediately with rice.

6 garlic cloves, minced

3 tablespoons gochugaru

1½ tablespoons mirin

½ teaspoon black pepper

2 tablespoons soy sauce

2 teaspoons kosher salt

1 14-ounce package of silken or extra-silken tofu, quartered

½ cup sliced fresh shiitake mushrooms

1 medium onion, cut into small dice

4 cups Anchovy Stock (page 195)

1 cup soy sauce

¼ cup mirin

¼ cup sake

Black pepper

½ cup peeled and chopped daikon radish

1 Asian pear, peeled, cored and sliced

1 red apple, peeled, cored and sliced

4 garlic cloves

4 pounds bone-in short ribs (see note, page 176)

1 teaspoon vegetable oil

Kosher salt

4 large Yukon Gold potatoes, peeled and roughly chopped

1 medium onion, quartered

1 medium carrot, cut into large dice

6 dried shiitake mushrooms, chopped

1 cup rice cakes (the disk-shaped variety used for soup)

1 cup Beef Stock (page 197)

# Crock-Pot Kalbijjim
## 갈비찜
### BEEF SHORT RIB STEW

This dish simply speaks to us—a recipe that uses traditional Korean flavors but with a preparation that is wholly American. The Crock-Pot was invented in 1971 by a Chicagoan named Irving Naxon, whose grandmother grew up eating slow-cooked cholent in her Lithuanian shtetl. With Naxon's electric slow cooker, a generation of Americans was raised on the culinary principal of "set it and forget it." This recipe has been created with just that in mind. After going low and slow for six hours, beef ribs become fall-off-the-bone tender while the vegetables glaze themselves in a robust, umami-rich sauce. There's natural sweetness from the apples and mirin and a savory edge from the soy sauce. It's a can't-miss combination.

For many Koreans, kalbijjim is considered a special-occasion dish, the one Mom makes to celebrate life's big achievements, like acing that calculus test or being named all state in tennis. This is because short ribs are expensive, especially in Korea. When preparing our version, it's important to take care with the initial sear on the ribs. Using the proper technique will pay dividends in the end, so fight the urge to flip quickly.

If you can plan ahead, we recommend that you make this the day before serving. Refrigeration will allow the fat to solidify at the top, which can then be spooned out easily. Reheat gently and you've got yourself a winning dish. And here's the move: Take it to a party and tell your friends it's beef stew. They probably will shrug because, really, who brings beef stew to a party? But the stew will be dispersed. Umami will speak. The party will listen. **SERVES 4 TO 6**

**I** In a food processor, blend the soy sauce, mirin, sake, 1 tablespoon black pepper, daikon radish, Asian pear, apple and garlic until smooth.

(recipe continues)

**2** Rub the short ribs with the vegetable oil and season with ample kosher salt and pepper. Set a large cast-iron skillet over high heat, and, when very hot, sear the ribs until golden-brown on all sides, 3 to 5 minutes per side. Only sear as many ribs as will fit comfortably in the pan; work in batches if necessary. Resist the urge to turn the meat before every surface has formed a crust. Drain the seared ribs of their fat.

**3** Place the seared meat at the bottom of an electric slow cooker. Add the potatoes, onion, carrot and mushrooms on top. Cover with a layer of rice cakes and then pour in the soy sauce mixture and Beef Stock. The sauce may have settled, so give it a good stir before pouring.

**4** Cook on the Crock-Pot's Low setting until the meat is fork tender and falls off the bone, about 6 hours. Serve with rice.

**ALTERNATIVELY, IF NOT USING A CROCK-POT:** If you're not down with the electric cooker, that is very much OK. Sear the meat in a Dutch oven, drain the fat, and layer in the vegetables, rice cakes, sauce and Beef Stock and bring to a boil. Reduce the heat to very low and simmer gently, stirring occasionally, until the meat is fork tender, about 2 hours.

### A NOTE ON BUYING SHORT RIBS

Short ribs are expensive, and rightly so: they are delicious and prized for their fat content and ability to get really tender. You can find quality bone-in short ribs at your local butcher shop or any Korean grocery store. Make sure there is a good meat-to-bone ratio; though Korean markets sometimes cut off a portion of the top to sell as boneless short ribs, there should be a thick slab of meat on top, even a good inch or two if you are lucky.

# Dakdoritang

## 닭도리탕

### SPICY CHICKEN STEW

In Korean stews, chicken is often overlooked, with beef, seafood and tofu receiving more play. One exception is dakdoritang, which incorporates gochujang and honey powder into the broth for a wonderfully spicy-sweet result. It's an absolutely delicious dish that can redefine your opinions about the limits of chicken stews. While you can cook the chicken directly in the broth for a softer, fattier result, we prefer adding a very worthwhile step: frying the thighs separately for a crispy texture.

When Deuki was studying at the Culinary Institute of America, he made dakdoritang for his Cuisines of Asia instructor, Michael Pardus (whom you may have read about in Michael Ruhlman's essential book *The Making of a Chef*). The stew had sweetness, underlying spice and pieces of perfectly fried chicken—basically everything Americans relish in a dish. Pardus loved it so much so that he included it in the curriculum. **SERVES 4**

**1 PREPARE THE STEW BASE:** In a large saucepan, combine the chicken stock, potato, onion, carrot, gochujang, honey powder, soy sauce, chile and garlic. Bring to a boil, then drop to a steady simmer and cook until the potatoes and carrots are tender, about 20 minutes.

**2 PREPARE THE CHICKEN:** Using paper towels, dry the chicken well, then season all over with the all-purpose flour and salt. Heat the oil in a large sauté pan over medium-high heat. When the oil shimmers, carefully place the chicken, skin side down, and top with a foil-wrapped brick, cast-iron pan or a heavy pot; cook for 10 minutes, spooning out some chicken fat and oil when it starts to render out and accumulate. (This prevents the skin from getting soggy.) When the skin side is golden brown and crisp, remove the weight, flip the chicken and cook until the juices run clear when poked with a knife, about 3 more minutes.

**3** Transfer the chicken to a plate lined with paper towels and let rest for 3 minutes. Slice the chicken into 1-inch strips and scatter atop the stew. Garnish with mushrooms, scallion and sesame seeds. Serve with rice.

### FOR THE STEW BASE

**3 cups chicken stock**

**1 medium russet potato, peeled and cut into large dice**

**1 medium onion, cut into large dice**

**1 medium carrot, cut into large dice**

**¼ cup gochujang**

**¼ cup honey powder or sugar**

**4 tablespoons soy sauce**

**1 green Korean or Anaheim chile, seeded and sliced**

**3 garlic cloves, minced**

### FOR THE CHICKEN

**1 pound boneless skin-on chicken thighs**

**2 tablespoons all-purpose flour**

**1 teaspoon kosher salt**

**3 tablespoons vegetable oil**

### FOR THE GARNISH

**2 ounces enoki mushrooms**

**1 scallion, thinly sliced**

**Sesame seeds**

# Seolleongtang
## 설렁탕
### BEEF BONE NOODLE SOUP

Seolleongtang is the deliciously beefy bone-broth soup that many Koreans eat at breakfast or to curb a night of excess—which is why you will often find it served at 24-7 restaurants. You can spot large cauldrons of the stuff bubbling in the back of a restaurant (some claim their burners have been going nonstop since Clinton was in office). After many hours of boiling, the oxtail should be stripped of most of its meat and marrow, which translates to a rich, though noticeably bland, broth. It sounds kind of odd, spending all that time to create a bland soup. But what happens next is the key: at the table, you add a healthy scoop of sea salt. It's amazing how the salt wakes up the rich marrow flavor of the beef. SERVES 4

1 In a large bowl or pot, submerge the oxtail bones in cold water for 1 hour to remove blood and bone shavings.

2 Drain and add the bones, 12 cups water, kombu, ginger and garlic to a stockpot. Bring to a boil over high heat and drop to a gentle simmer; cook, covered, for a total of 8 hours. This will be cooking for a long time, so check on it occasionally to make sure it doesn't rise to a full ripping boil. You also may need to add a little water along the way to keep everything submerged.

3 One hour before the boil is completed, add the daikon quarters and the beef brisket.

4 Meanwhile, boil the somen noodles as directed on the package, then immediately drain and shock them in cold water.

5 At the completion of the broth's cooking time, strain the broth through a fine mesh strainer, reserving the beef brisket and daikon. Discard the remaining solids.

6 To serve, divide the rice into 4 bowls. Top the rice with the somen noodles. Arrange the daikon and beef brisket on top. Pour the hot broth over the rice, noodles, daikon and brisket. Season with salt, pepper, gochugaru and scallions to taste.

4 pounds oxtail bones

12 cups water

1 3 × 3-inch square of kombu

3-inch knob of ginger

6 whole garlic cloves

1 daikon radish (about 1 pound), peeled and cut into quarters

1 pound beef brisket, shaved thin

1 bundle somen noodles

2 cups cooked rice

Sea or kosher salt to taste

Freshly ground black pepper

Gochugaru to taste

Sliced scallions to taste

2 pounds meaty pork neck bones

2 tablespoons vegetable oil

Kosher salt and black pepper

1 tablespoon gochugaru

1 tablespoon doenjang

1 tablespoon gochujang

2 tablespoons soy sauce

2 garlic cloves, minced

1 tablespoon mirin

6 tablespoons wild sesame seeds

4 cups Pork Stock (page 196) or water

2 large Yukon Gold potatoes, peeled and cut in half

1 Korean or Anaheim chile pepper, seeded and cut in half

½ bunch scallions, cut into 1-inch pieces

6 perilla or shiso leaves

FOR THE DIPPING SAUCE

3 tablespoons soy sauce

1 teaspoon grated horseradish or wasabi

1 teaspoon sugar

1 teaspoon Chinese mustard

1 tablespoon rice vinegar

# Gamjatang
## 감자탕

SPICY PORK NECK AND POTATO STEW

Myung San is a modest little twenty-seat restaurant located a short walk from the Broadway Long Island Rail Road station in Queens that was visited weekly by former New York Mets pitcher Jae Weong Seo. The reason was gamjatang, which literally means "potato soup" but is also a homonym for "pork neck soup." It's hardly just potato soup. While potato plays a role, the two key elements are meaty pork necks, cooked long until the meat is fall-off-the-bone amazing, and earthy, wild sesame seeds. Since these seeds are the key to the flavor of this stew, there is unfortunately no replacement. This unique flavor marriage inspired longtime Los Angeles restaurant critic, and gamjatang fan, Jonathan Gold to call the dish a Korean version of Oaxacan mole colorado. SERVES 4

1  Preheat oven to 475°F.

2  Place bones in a roasting pan and coat with vegetable oil. Season well with salt and pepper. Roast for 20 minutes until golden brown and well caramelized, flipping once halfway through.

3  While bones are roasting, combine gochugaru, doenjang, gochujang, soy sauce, garlic, mirin, 3 tablespoons wild sesame seeds and 1 teaspoon black pepper in a small bowl and whisk thoroughly, making sure the gochujang is well integrated. Set aside.

4  In a stockpot, combine the roasted bones, Pork Stock, potatoes, chile pepper, scallions and the gochugaru mixture and bring to a boil over medium-high heat before dropping to a simmer. Simmer for 45 minutes to 1 hour, partially covered.

5  Meanwhile, stir together all the ingredients for the dipping sauce in a small bowl until the sugar dissolves.

6  Once the flavors in the stockpot have mingled and the neck bones' meat is very tender, garnish the soup with perilla leaves and the remaining 3 tablespoons wild sesame seeds. Serve immediately with rice and dipping sauce on the side for the neck meat.

# EATING KOREATOWN
## LOS ANGELES RESTAURANT CRITIC JONATHAN GOLD

Pulitzer Prize–winning Jonathan Gold's last story as restaurant critic at *LA Weekly*, a post he held for nearly three decades, was a 10,973-word masterpiece detailing Korean food in Los Angeles. Though the "60 Korean Dishes Every Angeleno Should Know" headline reads more listicle than magnum opus, the article tells the story of not just where to get the most bomb-ass bossam in L.A. County—for the record, it's Kobawoo—but reaffirmed the nation's most-acclaimed restaurant critic as a keen observer and lover of Korean food and culture.

During the research of this book we followed Gold's lead to many of the sixty restaurants, including Hamji Park on West 6th Street—where we meet the critic on a warm February afternoon. We dive into grilled pork ribs, a steaming bowl of gamjatang and a small cauldron of cheonggukjang, an extra-fermented bean-paste soup that the critic compares, possibly

favorably, to *Invasion of the Body Snatchers*. "It just takes over your fucking system," he says, declining a bite. We start talking about his recent trip to South Korea, where he attended a kimchi festival and trucked around Gwangju with Oakland chef Russ Moore. "It's so obvious that Korea was such a profoundly poor country," he says after a sip of Chamisul soju. "They eat the low-tide stuff. There is hagfish and sea squirts off every coastline, but only a few will eat it. It's a cuisine of necessity."

And, as Gold describes it, necessity is the reason a vast number of L.A. Koreans moved to the city in the late '70s and early '80s, many to build businesses that make up the sprawling Koreatown of today. At that time, while the Korean economy slowly transitioned from an agrarian society to the technological superpower we know today, immigrants flowed into America's biggest cities in record numbers, hoping to make a better life for themselves. With few entrepreneurial opportunities, due to language barriers and cultural divides, many of the new arrivals opened food-related enterprises like produce markets, small grocery stores and, of course, restaurants that catered directly to the Korean American immigrant community. It was a "for us, by us" ethic that has remained strikingly the same, some thirty-some years later.

This may be why many Korean restaurants around America, but particularly in Los Angeles, tend to have a more dated aesthetic and a clear resistance to assimilate to Western tastes (for example, menus feature more Hangul than English, and Korean folk music plays on the crackly stereo).

"It's like if there was an 'American House' in another country and it was stuck in the Ed Koch era," notes the critic. But the lack of change presents a unique and downright exciting opportunity for people of all backgrounds to explore a food culture firmly of its time,

place and circumstances. And it's a reason we spent weeks in Los Angeles researching this book. It's a very special Koreatown.

"The thing is, the restaurants here are as good as the restaurants in Seoul," says Gold. He concedes that if you took the top fifty restaurants in both cities, the top ten would go to Seoul, but insists that numbers eleven through fifty would be in America.

While some *Korean* Koreans might question Gold's statement as hometown pride or ignorance, the truth of the matter is that Korean food in America is the real deal; in many cases it's never been watered down, and the tireless critic has spent a whole lot of time thinking about it.

We ask Gold to humor us with a bite of cheonggukjang. He dips his spoon into the funky stew and has a taste. "It's better on Olympic," he says. But we knew that already. It's in his article.

# Andong Jjimdak

## 안동찜닭

### SWEET SOY-BRAISED CHICKEN

Matt had never heard of Andong jjimdak when we found it at Yet Tuh in Doraville, Georgia. Restaurant critic Bill Addison has been visiting the tiny family-run business for years but also had skipped over this prized dish. But once the fragrant, communal plate of chicken arrived at table, we knew we were in for something special. The sauce is the key, based around the union of soy sauce, sugar, rice syrup, sake and oyster sauce. A handful of dried red chile peppers gives the sweetness a distinct kick.

Andong is a city located in east-central Korea, and some have traced the roots of this dish to a section of Andong Gu Market called Chicken Alley. It is there, they say, the dish was conceived in the 1980s as a way of competing with (or possibly joining) the growing Korean fried chicken craze (see page 141) that still remains today. Seoul food blogger Joe McPherson calls Chicken Alley the "beating heart of the best jjimdak in the world," while adding not to wear a white shirt while enjoying the messy, transportive dish. Back in Doraville, GA, we polished off the platter and talked about the city far across the ocean, all making plans to make our Chicken Alley pilgrimage sometime soon. **SERVES 4 TO 6**

**1** Lightly season chicken thighs all over with salt and pepper. In a small bowl, combine the soy sauce, mirin, sugar, rice syrup, oyster sauce, sake, sesame oil and 1 teaspooon black pepper.

**2** Set a large, high-sided sauté pan or Dutch oven on high heat and add the vegetable oil. Once the oil is lightly smoking, add the chicken, skin side down, and sear for 3 minutes, or until lightly browned. Flip and sear the other side for another 3 minutes, or until lightly browned.

**3** Add the potatoes, carrot, onion, scallion, garlic, cabbage and dried chiles, along with the soy sauce mixture and 1 cup of chicken stock. Bring to a boil and lower heat to gently simmer for 20 minutes, or until the vegetables are tender and the chicken is cooked through. Stir in vermicelli. Add more stock if needed to keep the dish saucy. Remove from heat. Taste and adjust seasoning with salt, pepper, soy sauce and sugar; you're looking for a balance of sweet, salty and spicy. Serve with sesame seeds.

---

**2 pounds chicken thighs or legs**

**Kosher salt and black pepper**

**⅓ cup soy sauce, plus more to taste**

**2 tablespoons mirin**

**¼ cup sugar, plus more to taste**

**1 tablespoon Korean rice or corn syrup**

**1 tablespoon oyster sauce**

**1 tablespoon sake**

**1½ tablespoons sesame oil**

**2 tablespoons vegetable oil**

**2 russet potatoes, peeled and cut into large dice**

**1 medium carrot, cut into large dice**

**1 medium onion, cut into large dice**

**4 scallions, trimmed**

**8 garlic cloves, minced**

**½ cup roughly chopped cabbage**

**8 dried Korean or Anaheim chile peppers**

**1½ cups chicken stock**

**1 cup dried sweet potato noodles, soaked in water for 30 minutes and drained**

**Sesame seeds, for garnish**

¼ cup sweet glutinous rice

1 young spring chicken or Cornish game hen

10 garlic cloves

4 dried jujubes or dried dates, cored

2 whole chestnuts, peeled

1 stalk of ginseng root, top cut off

1-inch knob of ginger, sliced

1 stalk of astragalus root, whole

1 scallion, white part only, and 1 scallion, thinly sliced, for garnish

5 cups chicken stock or water

Kosher salt and black pepper to taste

# Samgyetang
# 삼계탕
## GINSENG CHICKEN SOUP

For many non-Koreans, samgyetang poses a bit of a riddle. Why is a steaming hot chicken-and-rice soup eaten primarily in the hot and humid summer months? The answer rests not in the chicken but in the medicinal herbs that the dish is famous for. The idea is that during the sleepy summer months, people are in need of an energy boost—which ginseng and astragalus both provide, and which, to us, makes this soup a really delicious and fortifying recipe with interesting, aromatic, bitter-sweet flavors. Find a fresh young chicken or Cornish game hen and stuff it with sweet rice, Korean dates, chestnuts and the herbs. Cook it in the best possible chicken stock you can make or buy. Samgyetang is healthy and clean and might just be the answer the next time you need a pick-me-up, in summer or winter. SERVES 2 TO 4

1 Wash the rice and cover it with cold water for 30 minutes. Drain.

2 Rinse the chicken thoroughly in cold water. Stuff its cavity with the rice, 5 cloves of garlic, 2 jujubes, the chestnuts, the ginseng, and half the ginger. Set aside.

3 In a heavy stockpot, combine 5 cloves of garlic, 2 jujubes, the remaining ginger, astragalus root, scallion white and chicken stock. Place the chicken in the center of the pot. Bring the pot to a boil over medium-high heat, then immediately turn it down to low. Cover the pot with the lid and gently simmer for 1 hour.

4 When finished cooking, season to taste with salt and pepper. To serve, halve the chicken lengthwise, return it to the broth and garnish with the sliced scallion.

# EATING KOREATOWN
## FALL OUT BOY FRONTMAN PATRICK STUMP

"I love Korean food, and it's kind of like home to me." As a boy living in Glenview, a northern Chicago suburb with a vibrant Korean population, Patrick Stump grew up on pots of kimchi jjigae prepared by his best friend's mom. "When I eat something like bibimbap, I get that warm and fuzzy feeling," he says, misty eyed.

We've gathered in the heart of New York City's Koreatown, and Patrick, a recovering vegetarian, has found himself back on the sauce—well, the wheatgrass. So we've started at the city's best vegetarian restaurant, Hangawi, and the singer has asked for the heat as our server spoons the last of the gochujang into our sizzling dolsot bibimbap. Hangawi specializes in Korean "temple" cuisine, which translates to the meatless art of balancing yum and yang. Before heading into the humid night, it felt like we were leaving our own little private monastery—with an endless supply of OB beer and makgeolli.

The night, of course, was not over and we end up at the modest Muk Eun Ji, which is not on the Koreatown Star Maps. But what the street-level restaurant lacks in personality, it makes up for with a very special extra-mature kimchi that is flown in weekly from Jeonju, where the stuff has been made for more than 3,000 years.

Patrick orders the kimchi jeon, while we insist on a pot of budae jjigae. Known as army base stew, it's made by lacing a classic kimchi jjigae with hot dogs, Spam, ramyun noodles and American cheese. The kimchi jeon appears at the table, fried crispy with a funkiness that teeters on the line between transcendent and overpowering. Patrick is feeling it big time. And as we dive into the budae jjigae, swirling noodles around chunks of canned meat, we see our rock-star vegetarian eyeing the pot. "Fuck it, we're here to eat," he says, smiling, before taking a sip of Cass Light and biting into a tube steak. It tastes like home.

# Budae Jjigae
## 부대찌개
### SPICY ARMY BASE STEW

Often referred to as "army base stew," budae jjigae is a story of desperation and ingenuity born out of necessity during the Korean War. During that tumultuous time, impoverished Koreans were forced to use leftover U.S. army rations for sustenance, sometimes even foraging through trash piles in the process. Ever since, and in far happier times, this spicy stew bobbing with Uncle Sam's finest—Spam, hot dogs and processed American cheese—has remained in Korea's culinary orbit.

Today, budae jjigae is popular among young Koreans for another reason: its party-prolonging powers late at night. Head to Koreatown restaurants like Chunju Han-il Kwan in Los Angeles or Pocha 32 in New York City, and chances are you'll spot pots of jjigae (or a larger, more elaborate pot of jeongol) stationed at every other table. It's delicious and dead easy to prepare: just throw everything in a pot and let it bubble away. American cheese marrying with chile and ramen noodles with hunks of processed meat? You know that's going to work well. SERVES 4

1  In a large, shallow pot, whisk together ¼ cup Anchovy Stock with the gochugaru, garlic, mirin, soy sauce and sugar.

2  To the pot, add the Spam, hot dogs, rice cakes, kimchi, tofu, bean sprouts, mushrooms, bacon and onion. Pour 6 cups Anchovy Stock into the pot and bring to a boil over high heat. Reduce the heat to medium and simmer until the rice cakes are soft but maintain some bite, about 20 minutes. Season with salt and pepper to taste.

3  Add the ramyun noodles on top of the stew and cook for another 3 minutes. Top with the cheese slices and garnish with the scallion.

6¼ cups Anchovy Stock (page 195)

¼ cup plus 3 tablespoons gochugaru

5 garlic cloves, minced

¼ cup mirin

3 tablespoons soy sauce

2 tablespoons sugar

6 ounces Spam (½ a can), cut into large dice

2 beef hot dogs, thinly sliced

¾ cup frozen rice cakes, cut diagonally

1 cup medium-dice extra-fermented Napa Cabbage Kimchi (page 41)

8 ounces soft tofu, sliced ½ inch thick

1 cup bean sprouts

1 cup enoki mushrooms

3 strips smoked thick-cut bacon, cut into small dice

½ cup thinly sliced onions

Kosher salt and black pepper to taste

1 package Shin Ramyun Noodle Soup, or other instant noodle (noodles only)

2 slices of American cheese

1 scallion, sliced, for garnish

1 pound beef brisket

1½ medium onions,
1 quartered and ½ diced

6 whole garlic cloves,
plus 4 garlic cloves,
minced

1 cup peeled and
medium-dice daikon

2 quarts water

1 tablespoon sesame oil

¼ cup gochugaru

1 tablespoon doenjang

⅓ cup soy sauce

1 tablespoon kosher salt

1 teaspoon black pepper

3 scallions, cut into
2-inch batons

½ cup bean sprouts

½ cup water-packed
bracken fern, cut into
2-inch batons

1 medium zucchini,
peeled and cut into
medium dice

# Yukgaejang
## 육계장
### SPICY SHREDDED BEEF SOUP

Talk about the answer for a cold, or a cold afternoon. Yukgaejang is one of the spiciest soups you will find; even iron-bellied Koreans sometimes take a pass. It's also one of the beefiest soups you'll ever have, with a generous portion of shredded beef brisket. The dish is really simple to make and loaded with bracken fern, which is a soft and noodle-like vegetable that can be found at Asian grocery stores—typically packed in water. You can also use dried bracken; just put it in a bowl and cover it with water for a couple hours beforehand to rehydrate it. **SERVES 4**

1  In a stockpot, place beef, the quartered onion, 6 garlic cloves, ½ cup of the diced daikon and 2 quarts of water. Heat on high and bring to a boil, then drop the heat to a simmer for 45 minutes. Strain, reserving the brisket and stock and discarding the vegetables. Allow the brisket to cool in the stock. When cool enough to handle, shred the brisket.

2  Add sesame oil to a large saucepan and heat on high until smoking. Stir in the gochugaru and immediately turn off the heat; this releases the oil from the dried chile flakes. Add the doenjang, soy sauce, minced garlic, salt and black pepper and stir to combine.

3  To the same pan, add the scallions, bean sprouts, diced onion, remaining ½ cup daikon, bracken fern and zucchini, along with the reserved stock and brisket, and bring to a boil over high heat. Once bubbling, serve immediately.

# Kongbiji Jjigae
## 콩비지찌개
### GROUND SOYBEAN SOUP

There are cozy little restaurants situated along Olympic Boulevard in Los Angeles or Buford Highway outside Atlanta, usually decorated with homey wooden furnishings and traditional Korean tchotchkes, that are masters in the art of tofu. Here, freshly made bean curd is manipulated into a host of bubbling stews called jjigae, the smooth, creamy tofu a palette for meats, kimchis, chiles or other flavors. One of the greatest dishes that comes out of this style of restaurants is kongbiji jjigae—a thick, porridge-like soup that is made from the puree of soaked soybeans. Our version is nuttier than Soondubu Jjigae (page 173) and served with chunks of pork shoulder and kimchi. It's a real stick-to-your-ribs dish that we made several times during the repressive winter we experienced while writing this book. **SERVES 4**

**1 cup dried soybeans**

**2 garlic cloves, minced**

**½-inch knob of ginger, minced**

**2 teaspoons sesame oil**

**Kosher salt to taste**

**½ teaspoon freshly cracked black pepper**

**½ pound pork shoulder, cut into medium dice**

**½ cup medium-dice extra-fermented kimchi**

1  Soak the soybeans in 6 cups of water at room temperature for 6 hours to overnight. Drain.

2  In a medium saucepan, cover the beans with 1 quart of fresh water and bring to a boil over high heat, then boil for 10 minutes. Drain, reserving the liquid. Shock the soybeans in a bowl of cold water, then rub the soybeans together to loosen the skins; remove and discard the skins. In a food processor or a blender, process the boiled soybeans until they are a coarse puree.

3  In a small bowl, mix together the garlic, ginger, sesame oil, a few pinches of salt and the black pepper. Add the pork and kimchi and combine.

4  Heat a large saucepan over medium heat. When hot, add the kimchi-pork mixture. Cook for 3 minutes, until fragrant. Add 3 cups of the reserved soybean water and salt to taste and bring to a boil. Once boiling, add 2 cups of the blended soybean mixture and return to a boil. Season to taste with salt and serve immediately.

**1 ounce dried seaweed (sold as miyeok or wakame)**

**6 cups water**

**1 3 × 3-inch square of kombu**

**¼ pound beef brisket, thinly sliced**

**2 tablespoons soy sauce**

**2 garlic cloves, minced**

**Sesame oil to taste**

# Miyeokguk
## 미역국
### BIRTHDAY SEAWEED SOUP

Miyeokguk is a light, slightly briny beef-and-seaweed soup that is commonly served to new mothers for its great health benefits—the broth is packed with antioxidants and omega-3 fatty acids, and if you eat this you will live to be 100. Even if you aren't looking for near immortality, the soup is swimming with umami, simple to make and super satisfying: the miyeok (also sold under its Japanese name, wakame) is pleasantly chewy, and small bits of beef brisket bob around in the broth for a nice textural component. Koreans love this stuff so much that it is commonly served on birthdays. Wait, no Fudgie the Whale ice cream cake? This ties back to the new-mother thing. You know how your mom gets all emo on your birthday, calling to tell you about the time she took you home from the hospital? Well, Korean moms make soup. Deuki cannot remember a birthday gone by that his mother hasn't asked him if he's had his bowl (or three) of miyeokguk. **SERVES 2**

1 Rehydrate seaweed by fully submerging it in a bowl of cold water for 30 minutes. Drain.

2 While the seaweed is rehydrating, combine the square of kombu and 6 cups water in a medium saucepan. Set over high heat and boil for 15 minutes. Remove and discard the kombu.

3 To the kombu broth, add the rehydrated seaweed, beef, soy sauce and garlic; gently simmer over medium-low heat for 10 minutes. Add a couple drops of sesame oil to taste. Serve.

# Myeolchi Yooksoo
## 멸치육수
### ANCHOVY STOCK

This quick-cooking stock can be the base for virtually every soup and stew in the Korean kitchen. You see water listed as an ingredient for a recipe? This light stock will make it better, deeper and packed with umami. Accordingly, you will find this stock used throughout the book, so if you'd like, make a large batch and freeze it in portions.

Finding quality dried anchovies is as easy as finding an Asian supermarket: the skin should look healthy, more silvery than gray, and the best ones to use for stock are at least 2 inches long. (If you're really into convenience, you can buy anchovy-stock packages, which resemble large tea bags; their flavor isn't quite as nuanced as our recipe, but they'll do in a pinch.) Removing the guts is a perfectionist step and something Deuki favors because it leads to a cleaner-tasting product, but it's not strictly necessary. To do so, use your fingers to pull out the black middle section so that only the fish's head and spine remains.

Dashima is better known by its Japanese name: kombu. It's sold in dried sheets that are typically coated in a white powder. Do not wash this off—it aids in delivering glutamates to the stock. That's natural MSG, people! Finally, make sure to watch the clock on this, as overboiling will dampen the stock's potency. **MAKES 1 QUART**

1 In a medium saucepan, combine 1 quart water, anchovies, daikon, scallions, kombu and chiles. Bring to a gentle simmer over medium-high heat, then lower heat to maintain a simmer for 15 minutes.

2 Strain the mixture into a medium container using a mesh strainer and discard the solids. The broth should have a cloudy, light caramel color with a deep sea taste and a slight kick from the chile peppers. Use the stock immediately, cool and refrigerate for a couple days or freeze for up to 2 months.

**1 quart water**

**25 dried anchovies**

**¼ cup roughly chopped daikon**

**1 bunch of scallions, trimmed and cut into thirds**

**2 2 × 2-inch squares of kombu (aka dashima)**

**2 jalapeño peppers or Anaheim chiles, halved lengthwise**

3 pounds pork neck
bones

1 gallon water

½ bunch of scallions,
sliced into 1-inch pieces

2 whole garlic cloves

1 tablespoon doenjang

1-inch knob of ginger

# Doaejigogi Yooksoo
## 돼지고기육수
### PORK STOCK

As with any soup or stew, using water is good but using stock is better. This simple pork-stock recipe incorporates the fermented bean paste doenjang, which adds an extra layer of flavor. **MAKES ABOUT 3 QUARTS**

1  Add pork bones and 1 gallon of water to a large stockpot and bring to a boil over high heat. Drop the heat to maintain a gentle simmer and continue cooking, covered, for 2 hours, skimming off any fat or foam as needed.

2  Add scallions, garlic, doenjang and ginger and continue to simmer for 1 more hour, uncovered. Strain the stock into a container and let it cool to room temperature before refrigerating. The stock keeps for a week in the refrigerator and for months frozen.

# Sogogi Yooksoo
## 소고기육수
### BEEF STOCK

This beef stock gets its Korean character with the inclusion of garlic, ginger and Korean green onions, which are longer and thicker at the root than grocery-store scallions; you can find these at Asian grocery stores. Beef stock can be used in Seolleongtang (page 179), Haejangguk (page 160) and Doenjang Jjigae (page 170). **MAKES 2 QUARTS**

**2 pounds oxtail bones**

**14 cups water**

**1-inch knob of ginger**

**5 whole garlic cloves**

**3 green onions or leeks, whites only**

1 Soak oxtail bones in cold water for 1 hour, which will remove blood and bone fragments. Lift the bones from the water and drain.

2 Fill a stockpot with the beef bones, 14 cups of water, ginger, garlic and green onions.

3 Bring the water to a boil over high heat, then lower to a simmer for 6 to 8 hours; keep the pot covered. Occasionally check on it to make sure the bones are covered with water and skim off any fat.

4 Strain stock into a container and let it cool to room temperature before refrigerating. Stock keeps for a week in the refrigerator and for months frozen.

# Respect:
# Guest Recipes

존경

**E**arly on, when we started conducting the research for this book, it became clear that a lot of our friends in the chef world—from a whole bunch of different backgrounds—were almost universally becoming more and more informed by Asian flavors. No longer did a chef have to be cooking full-steam Japanese to use togarashi, or be creating a special Chinese menu to bring the tingly awesomeness of Szechuan peppercorns to their nightly special. Today, Asian flavors are hybridizing modern cuisine. It's not "fusion." It's bigger than that, as these cultures have just become an everyday part of our culinary language. And Korean flavors and ingredients, in particular, have excited many of our heroes.

This chapter represents a respect so many chefs have for the Korean larder—using products like gochujang, yuzucha and dried seaweed in both traditional and nontraditional ways. We see respect for the Korean culture, and some of the chefs featured have visited Korea, employ Koreans in their kitchens or have a trusted Korean best friend (KBF). These recipes are from chefs representing all styles of cooking around the United States. There are haute-vegetarian chefs and out-of-the-box sandwich artists. There are meat mavens, James Beard award winners and fixtures of the Michelin Guide.

As for the recipes, we think they're pretty inspired. There's raw fish seasoned with the flavors of kalbi, and pork belly braised with doenjang. Kimchis are present, of course, which reflects modern cooking's growing love affair with fermentation. But there's also Korean fried broccoli and chicken wings marinated in gochujang and Coca-Cola.

Why have these flavors and techniques inspired everybody from Eric Ripert to Paul Qui to Sean Brock? Sure, gochujang has been called the next sriracha and is one powerful condiment. And substituting kombu and anchovy stock for chicken or beef stock can add a unique twist. But simply put, Korea is going to play a major role in the future of cooking in America. And the best of the best chefs always want to be one step ahead. So why not get in there and start being the future too? 끝

2 teaspoons gochujang

2 teaspoons Kewpie Mayonnaise

4 King's Hawaiian Sweet Rolls, split

4 3 × 3-inch sheets of toasted nori seaweed

¼ pound Cowgirl Creamery Mt Tam cheese, thinly sliced

1 small Granny Smith apple, cored and thinly sliced

¼ pound Napa Cabbage Kimchi (page 41)

½ tablespoon butter

# Kimchi Triple-Cream Grilled Cheese

## BY PAUL QUI

In Austin, Texas, chef Paul Qui is the winner of an unprecedented trifecta of culinary honors: *Top Chef* champion, *Food & Wine* magazine's Best New Chef honoree and winner of the James Beard Foundation Award for Best Restaurant: Southwest for his work at experimental sushi den Uchiko. The Beard awards are sorta like the Oscars of the food world, and Paul Qui is a Ben Affleck figure, a winner in front of the camera *and* behind it. Qui also owns and operates the restaurant Qui and a fleet of popular food trucks called East Side Kings, where this dish is served.

The fluffy Hawaiian sweet roll is pretty much the perfect bread choice for a grilled-cheese slider, especially one that bridges the gastronomy of Korea with badass triple-cream cheeses. For those without access to King's Hawaiian rolls or cheese from San Francisco's famed Cowgirl Creamery, you can substitute miniature potato rolls and a good triple cream like Camembert. SERVES 2

1 In a small bowl, stir the gochujang and mayonnaise to combine. Spread the mixture evenly on the 8 roll halves. Divide the nori, cheese, apple and kimchi among the roll bottoms. Close sandwiches with the remaining roll tops.

2 Preheat a large skillet over medium heat. Add the butter and swirl the pan. When the butter foams, cook the sandwiches until golden brown, 2 to 3 minutes on each side. Serve immediately.

# Korean Fried Broccoli

## BY AMANDA COHEN

Amanda Cohen's Dirt Candy is a vegetarian restaurant, sure. But it's more of a *vegetable* restaurant, avoiding meat proxies like veggie burgers and wheat balls. "We do not care what you eat before, or after, the meal—we just want you to come enjoy the vegetables for this one moment," says Cohen in her maple syrup–thick Canadian accent. And, indeed, people enjoy those vegetables. Since 2008, the New York City restaurant has been perpetually packed. As somebody who has lived near Manhattan's Koreatown for many years, Cohen's always thinking about ways to incorporate the flavors into her menus (her kimchi donuts were a longtime hit). With this broccoli, she adds her touch by smoking before battering and frying. Trust us, it's so worth the extra step. The sauce brings out the umami cannons with black rice vinegar, soy sauce and brown sugar. SERVES 4 TO 6

1  **MAKE THE SAUCE:** Mix together all sauce ingredients in a big bowl and reserve at room temperature.

2  **MAKE THE BROCCOLI:** Smoke the broccoli either by using a smoker or constructing one with foil: Line a deep baking pan with a double-layer of foil, add hickory chips to cover the bottom and soak the chips in water to cover for 1 hour. Drain well. Place the broccoli on a plate or tray that can later fit inside the the baking pan on a rack (to keep them off the chips). Cover the pan with more foil, like a lid. Place the pan over high heat. Once smoke starts to curl out from under the lid, take it off the heat, carefully remove the foil lid and place the rack and tray of broccoli over the chips. Re-cover and turn the heat back on high. When smoke comes out from under the lid again, turn off the heat and remove the broccoli from the pan.

3  Heat 4 inches of vegetable oil in a heavy pot or Dutch oven with high sides and affix a frying thermometer to the side of the pot. Turn the heat on low. You want the oil at 375°F; the low heat buys you time to continue prepping, but check on the temperature occasionally.

(recipe continues)

### FOR THE SAUCE

**2 garlic cloves, minced**

**2 teaspoons minced ginger**

**2 tablespoons plus 2 teaspoons soy sauce**

**¼ cup gochujang**

**2 tablespoons black rice vinegar**

**2 tablespoons plus 1 teaspoon sesame oil**

**2 teaspoons brown sugar**

### FOR THE BROCCOLI

**1½ pounds broccoli florets**

**Vegetable oil, for frying**

**¾ cup cornstarch**

**1¼ teaspoons baking powder**

**2 tablespoons panko bread crumbs**

**1 teaspoon kosher salt**

**½ cup all-purpose flour**

**½ cup ice-cold vodka**

**½ cup ice-cold seltzer**

**1 tablespoon toasted sesame seeds**

**¼ cup thinly sliced scallions**

Special equipment: smoker or a deep baking pan; rack and tray that fit inside the baking pan; a handful of hickory or other wood chips; frying thermometer

**4** In a medium bowl, toss the smoked broccoli in ¼ cup of the cornstarch, then shake off the excess powder.

**5** Mix the remaining cornstarch, baking powder, panko, salt and all-purpose flour together in a large bowl. Add vodka and seltzer to the cornstarch mixture and mix just to combine.

**6** Roll the broccoli in the wet batter and line a tray with paper towels.

**7** Adjust the heat to reach 375°F. Over medium-high heat, carefully transfer the broccoli to the fryer, a few pieces at a time, just enough to fit comfortably in the oil without crowding the pot. Fry the broccoli until golden brown. Remove with a slotted spoon and set on paper towels to drain.

**8** Toss the broccoli in the sauce. Sprinkle with sesame seeds and scallions and serve.

FOR THE BRISKET
AND BROTH

**1 beef brisket, untrimmed, about 10 pounds**

**Kosher salt**

**10 pounds beef marrow bones**

**1 large onion, cut into large dice**

**1 pound daikon radish, peeled and cut into 1-inch rounds**

**1 5 × 5-inch square of kombu**

FOR SERVING

**8 ounces sea urchin**

**½ cup thinly sliced chives**

**1 cup Radish Kimchi (page 40)**

**Fish sauce**

**8 ounces cured trout roe (salmon roe or ikura is a fine substitute)**

**Korean sea salt**

**Black pepper**

# Seolleongtang with Smoked Brisket and Sea Urchin

## BY DANNY BOWIEN

This is an amped-up version of one of Danny Bowien's favorite soups. "My first experience with seolleongtang was magical," says the chef of Mission Chinese Food, who was was born in Korea and adopted by an Oklahoma family as an infant. After discovering Korean food while living in San Francisco as a young adult, Bowien finally returned to his birthland with his Korean-born wife, Youngmi. "I was jet-lagged and starving, and woke up at my in-laws to a bowl of this soup that had this rich, beefy stock but was so clean and restorative. Pure magic."

This recipe is pretty true to the original, with a long-simmered bone broth that tastes of beefiness and marrow. But there are also a couple curve balls, typical of the chef's multicultural mash-up style. Smoked beef brisket adds a unique depth of flavor and a tip of the ten-gallon to Texas (we've included the instructions to smoke at home, but to save time you can always buy from your favorite barbecue spot or skip the smoking altogether). Seolleongtang is traditionally made without seasoning, a palm full of powdery salt added tableside. Bowien adds complexity by using fish sauce and cured trout roe. Sea urchin is added at the end. Baller. And note, this recipe makes a ton of brisket, and you will have leftovers. Not a bad thing. SERVES 8 TO 12

1  Two days before preparation, separate the lean, flat end from the fatty "point" end of the brisket. Rub both pieces generously with kosher salt and allow them to cure on a rack, refrigerated and uncovered, overnight.

2  The next day, set up a smoker with cherry or apple wood and smoke the fatty (point end) of the brisket for 9 hours at 212°F. The brisket should be very tender and give easily when pressed with a knife. Wrap in parchment and allow it to cool to room temperature, then wrap in plastic and refrigerate.

**3** While the brisket smokes, place the bones in a large stockpot and cover with cold water. Bring to a boil over high heat, then strain, discarding the water. Rinse the bones in cold water, then replace them in the pot. Combine the onion and daikon with the kombu, bones and the lean (flat) end of brisket in the pot. Cover with plenty of water and bring to a simmer over high heat, then reduce heat to maintain a gentle simmer. Cook, uncovered, for about 1 hour, until the radish is tender. Remove the radish and brisket from the pot and transfer them to a shallow container. Top with just enough broth to cover and allow them to cool in liquid, then refrigerate.

**4** Continue to cook the broth, uncovered, for 8 hours, making sure that the bones are always covered with water; replenish the water when necessary. The broth should taste very rich; it's OK if it's a bit bland, because you will season it at the table.

**5** Strain the broth and let cool, discarding the solids. Refrigerate overnight.

**6** The next day, skim any fat that has solidified on the surface of the broth. Thinly slice both the simmered and smoked brisket and let them sit until they reach room temperature, or gently warm them, covered, in a 250°F oven. Bring the broth to a simmer and add the reserved daikon and thinly sliced lean brisket.

**7** Serve the soup in bowls, topped with sea urchin and chives, with the sliced smoked brisket and radish kimchi alongside; let guests season to taste with fish sauce, roe, sea salt and pepper.

1 teaspoon grated ginger

1 garlic clove, minced

3 tablespoons brown
sugar

3 tablespoons soy sauce

3 tablespoons rice
vinegar

2 tablespoons sesame oil

¼ pound raw sushi-grade
hamachi, sliced ⅛-inch
thick

Kosher salt

¼ teaspoon gochugaru

1 teaspoon chopped
cilantro

1 tablespoon finely diced
apple (tart apple, like
Pink Lady, preferred)

2 small radishes, sliced
thinly into rounds

1 handful mung bean
sprouts, for garnish

1 handful radish
or broccoli sprouts
(optional)

# Raw Hamachi Crudo with Kalbi Vinaigrette

## BY VINNY DOTOLO AND JON SHOOK

Vinny Dotolo and Jon Shook run several highly successful restaurants in Los Angeles including Animal, Son of a Gun and Trois Mec with chef Ludo Lefebvre. While Animal does kung pao sweetbreads and oxtail poutine with a wink, nudge and serious cooking chops, Son of a Gun serves as a tribute to the seafood shack fare the pair grew up on back in Florida—and also where they've served a plate of raw hamachi dressed with apples, cilantro and an ingenious flavors-of-kalbi vinaigrette. Like L.A. chefs of all backgrounds, Koreatown is woven into the fabric of their kitchen existence and this dish serves as an appropriate tribute. So find some good "sashimi-grade" hamachi at your favorite fishmonger (tuna or fluke will also work) and make a batch of this quick dressing, which will also work well on salad greens if you have some left over. **SERVES 2**

**1  MAKE THE VINAIGRETTE:** Add the ginger and garlic to a blender with the brown sugar, soy sauce and vinegar. Blend until smooth. Transfer to a mixing bowl and whisk in sesame oil until fully incorporated.

**2**  Divide the sliced fish onto 2 plates. Sprinkle with salt, to taste, and gochugaru. Spoon 1 tablespoon vinaigrette onto each plate of fish. Scatter the cilantro, apple, radish, bean sprouts and radish sprouts, if using, over the fish and serve.

2 tablespoons unsalted butter

2 tablespoons sesame oil

½-inch knob of ginger, minced

¼ cup thinly sliced scallions, plus more for garnish

1 tablespoon sambal oelek or gochugaru

1 cup roughly chopped Napa Cabbage Kimchi (page 41)

6 ounces fresh yuba, cut into 1-inch strips

4 eggs, poached

¼ cup Kimchi Vinaigrette (see opposite)

¼ cup Daikon Radish Kimchi (page 40)

¼ pound Dungeness crabmeat, cooked (optional)

# Spicy Kimchi Yuba "Noodles" With Poached Egg

## BY STUART BRIOZA

The question of Stuart Brioza's love of kimchi is answered with a trip up a wobbly ladder to a secret loft space turned fermentation lab above his insanely popular San Francisco restaurant, State Bird Provisions. In this crawl space, we spotted large buckets of napa cabbage and daikon radish kimchi, which the chef makes year-round using chopped-up Beausoleil oysters. "I'm a Bay Area kid, so the idea of mixing cultures comes naturally to me," he says, sipping an espresso in the restaurant's sunny dining room. We're talking about the marriage of Japanese yuba—the delicate skin that forms on top of soy milk while making tofu—with Korean kimchi, a dish he has served since the early days of State Bird, and one that has become one of the restaurants' signatures.

Brioza was nice enough to slip us the recipe, and we've made it many times since. Whenever we can find fresh yuba, sold at Asian supermarkets, we have this relatively simple recipe top of mind. The inviting, fragile-but-chewy texture of the tofu skin and the richness of the egg yolk are beautifully contrasted with a burst of Kimchi Vinaigrette (recipe follows). It's easy to make, but also slightly chef-y and out of the box. And if you happen to be reading this during Dungeness crab season, it's a great addition at the end. SERVES 4 AS AN APPETIZER

1 Heat a large sauté pan over medium-high heat and add butter and sesame oil. When the butter has fully melted, add the ginger, scallions and sambal oelek and cook until fragrant, about 30 seconds.

2 Add the chopped kimchi and yuba and sauté for 1 minute, just enough to heat through and combine the flavors.

3 Divide the yuba mixture onto 4 plates. Top each with a poached egg. Garnish with Kimchi Vinaigrette, Daikon Radish Kimchi and scallions. Divide the Dungeness crab, if using, among the plates and serve.

## KIMCHI VINAIGRETTE

Stuart Brioza uses this dressing as a way to add a layer of freshness when working with rich flavors. In addition to the spicy kimchi-yuba recipe opposite, the dressing also works well with pork belly, grilled squid, avocado or anything that can use a hit of savory tartness. **MAKES 1½ CUPS**

**1 cup kimchi juice**

**1 garlic clove, finely grated**

**1-inch knob of ginger, finely grated**

**3 tablespoons fish sauce**

**¼ cup grapeseed oil**

**2 tablespoons sesame oil**

Whisk together kimchi juice, garlic, ginger, fish sauce, grapeseed oil and sesame oil. Will keep in the refrigerator for up to 2 weeks.

½ teaspoon fine sea salt

⅛ teaspoon xanthan gum

Pinch of sugar

½ teaspoon Espelette
pepper

¼ cup lemon juice

1 teaspoon thinly sliced
garlic

1 tablespoon gochujang

¼ cup extra-virgin
olive oil

FOR THE BBQ SAUCE

1 tablespoon sliced
garlic

1 teaspoon sliced ginger

¼ cup grated onion
(about ¼ small onion)

¼ cup white miso paste

½ cup gochujang

¼ cup Japanese rice
vinegar

2 tablespoons mirin

2 tablespoons soy sauce

½ teaspoon sesame oil

FOR THE KIMCHI-STYLE
VEGETABLES

Kosher salt

12 baby bok choy,
trimmed

4 napa cabbage leaves,
kept long but ends
trimmed

# Korean Surf and Turf: Escolar with BBQ Beef and Kimchi-Style Vegetables
## BY ERIC RIPERT

Even before acclaimed New York City chef and TV guy Eric Ripert visited Korea with Matt (see page 212), he had experimented with fusing the flavors of Korean barbecue and kimchi with his delicate seafood cookery. Long on the Le Bernardin tasting menu, this advanced recipe includes a kimchi marinade, homemade barbecue sauce and citrus-soy emulsion, as well as separate techniques for grilling escolar, one of the chef's favorite fishes, and pan-searing strip steaks. But we really think the sink full of pots and pans is worth the final result: a composed Korean surf and turf that will impress your friends at your next Saturday night dinner party. Eric's got your back. **SERVES 4**

**1 MAKE THE KIMCHI MARINADE:** Mix together the salt, xanthan gum, sugar and Espelette and set aside. In a blender, combine lemon juice, garlic and gochujang. Slowly drizzle in the extra-virgin olive oil to emulsify, then add the dry ingredients and emulsify. Refrigerate until ready to use.

**2 MAKE THE BBQ SAUCE:** Combine all of the ingredients in a blender until smooth and pass through a fine strainer. Refrigerate until ready to use.

**3 PREPARE THE KIMCHI VEGETABLES:** Set a medium pot of water to boil with enough salt to make it pleasantly salty. Fill a bowl with ice water and set it nearby. Blanch the baby bok choy for 1 minute, until bright green and slightly softened. Immediately chill in the ice water, drain, and hold at room temperature. Blanch the napa cabbage leaves for 30 seconds in the boiling water and immediately plunge them into the ice-water bath. Dry the leaves really well. Save the largest napa cabbage leaf and set aside. Take the remaining cabbage leaves and slice them in ¼-inch strips. Mix the strips of cabbage with 3 tablespoons of the kimchi marinade and salt to taste. Lay the large whole napa cabbage leaf out and lay the cabbage strips on top. Roll the large leaf around the kimchi, forming a tight, even roll. Slice the roll into 12 bite-size pieces. Set aside at room temperature.

**4 MAKE THE CITRUS SOY EMULSION:** Bring 2 tablespoons water, the soy sauce and the citrus juices to a simmer over medium heat in a small saucepan. Turn the heat down to low and whisk in the butter, one piece at a time, forming a smooth sauce. Keep sauce warm, off direct heat.

**5 COOK THE FISH:** Preheat a grill, or a grill pan on the stove, to medium-high heat. With a paper towel, grease the grates with 1 teaspoon grapeseed oil. Season the escolar on both sides with salt and pepper. Grill the escolar, about 1 minute per side, to medium-rare in the center.

**6 COOK THE BEEF:** Heat a medium sauté pan over medium-high heat with 2 teaspoons of oil. Season the beef on both sides with salt and pepper. Brush 1 teaspoon BBQ sauce on each portion, coating both sides. When the oil is shimmering-hot, sear the beef in the pan, about 1 minute per side, turning them once, so that each side is browned and the meat is medium.

**7** Arrange the kimchi roll slices (3 per plate) on the top half of each plate. In a large sauté pan set over medium-high heat, quickly warm the blanched baby bok choy with a splash of water for steam, and mix with a little kimchi marinade. Arrange a baby bok choy next to each kimchi roll. Draw a thin line of BBQ sauce horizontally across the bottom half of each plate. Place a piece of beef over the BBQ sauce. Place a piece of escolar offset and slightly overlapping the beef on each plate. Arrange 3 Asian pear matchsticks on top of each piece of escolar. Spoon the citrus soy emulsion over the fish. Voilà.

FOR THE CITRUS SOY EMULSION

**2 tablespoons soy sauce**

**1 lemon, juiced and strained**

**1 lime, juiced and strained**

**4 tablespoons unsalted butter, cut into 4 chunks**

FOR THE ESCOLAR

**1 teaspoon grapeseed or vegetable oil**

**1 escolar fillet (10 ounces), cut into 4 portions**

**Fine sea salt and freshly ground white pepper**

FOR THE BEEF

**2 teaspoons grapeseed or vegetable oil**

**1 New York strip steak (8 ounces), cut into 4 portions**

**Fine sea salt and freshly ground black pepper**

**½ Asian pear, peeled, cored and cut into thick matchsticks**

# Q&A
## ERIC RIPERT REALLY LIKES KOREA, WE REALLY LIKE ERIC RIPERT

In fall 2013, Matt and Eric Ripert traveled throughout Korea for a *Bon Appétit* story. Ripert, chef-owner of the three-Michelin-star seafood restaurant Le Bernardin in New York City, dove nose first into the country's grand traditions in fermentation, while combing the country's live fish markets for all sorts of seafood.

---

Inspired, Ripert visited the country again in 2014, this time bringing along a film crew to tape his television show, *Avec Eric*. The chef, a practicing Buddhist who considers the Dalai Lama a personal teacher, is deeply interested in the foods of the Korean temples, which serve as a contrast to the fire and pickling of classic Korean cooking. At temples, five "overpowering" vegetables (onions, garlic, green onions, chives and leeks), called oshinchae, are effectively banned because they alter the focus needed for spiritual practice. Matt chatted with the chef about his trips to the peninsula, discovering the country's range of cooking and his growing love of all things Korea.

### What draws you to Korean cuisine and culture?

Korean cuisine is very convivial. Very flavorful. And no one is scared of eating garlic and spices, and I like that very much! I don't like to make comparisons between cultures, but if Japan were French, Korea would be Italian. Korean is full of flavor and in your face. Though in France we love stinky cheese, and we don't care if the Germans think we are barbarians. The Koreans are the same.

### Yeah, Korean cuisine has a lot of in-your-face qualities. It's very rough. It's got a lot of guts.

To me it's the quintessential soul food from Asia. Everybody eats around the table, and shares and shares and shares. This is very special.

### Korea is a country of 3,000 miles of coastline. What did you think about the seafood?

What is so interesting about Korea is that, obviously seafood is present everywhere, and the diet is so centered around it. But when you go to the markets, what I was very impressed with were the live fish that were caught wild and kept alive in tanks. You go to Hong Kong and you find farm-raised tuna, live in bags. But in Korea, you find it alive and straight from the ocean. You don't find that in the Western world.

### That impresses you.

To get fish live is amazing. Sometimes you have to actually let the fish rest; you cannot eat it right away because it is too firm. But you have the luxury to decide what you want do.

**And what about gochujang?**

Gochujang is a magical ingredient. When you think about it, you make anything with gochujang and it tastes good (*laughs*).

**Would you ever open a restaurant in Seoul?**

No, because I don't want to open restaurants. I don't want to work more than I do. But if I did want to work more than I do, I would open in Korea, yes.

2 liters Coca-Cola

1 cup spicy gochujang

½ cup Thai green curry paste (Maesri brand is a good choice)

2-inch knob of ginger, minced

3 garlic cloves, coarsely chopped

¼ cup fish sauce

2 pounds boneless, skin-on chicken thighs

Kosher salt and black pepper

Cola and Gochujang Barbecue Sauce, warmed (recipe follows)

# Coca-Cola and Gochujang-Marinated Chicken Thighs

## BY JAMIE BISSONNETTE

While the flavor of the Mediterranean is what earned chef Jamie Bissonnette high praise at his Boston and New York City restaurants Coppa and Toro, it's his inventive use of Asian ingredients that has really grabbed our attention. A few years back, Matt judged a nose-to-tail pork-cooking competition called Grand Cochon, and Bissonnette, inspired by a three-week trip to Vietnam, served five incredible dishes, including lemongrass sausage and red curried pig skin. Matt still dreams of that afternoon. Bissonnette has also long been a fan of Korean ingredients—he's been mainlining doenjang and gochujang since his early cooking days in Boston.

This is a simple meat marinade the chef uses on his menu at Toro. It works beautifully with beef cuts like hanger, skirt and flank, with pork belly or even fatty grilled fish, like a hamachi collar. But his favorite use by far is chicken thighs. The base is Coca-Cola and spicy gochujang, giving the meat a pronounced sweetness, but with balanced acidity and complexity. Its chunky barbecue-sauce cousin is just as interesting, used either as sauce on the side or for a quick finishing brush on the grill, and it will hold in the fridge for weeks. SERVES 4

1 Whisk together the Coca-Cola, gochujang, curry paste, ginger, garlic and fish sauce in a large mixing bowl until combined.

2 Place the chicken in a sealable container, pour the marinade over the chicken to cover and marinate in the refrigerator for 4 hours to overnight. (Any extra marinade keeps in the fridge for 1 week.)

3 Remove chicken from marinade and pat very dry with paper towels. Season chicken with salt and pepper.

**4** Preheat the broiler on the lower setting, if available, or place the oven rack at least 8 inches from the heating element. Place chicken, skin side down, on a rack set in a baking sheet and broil chicken until it begins to brown, about 5 minutes. Flip the chicken and broil the skin side until cooked through, about 20 minutes longer. Keep an eye on the chicken as it cooks; if the skin starts to darken too quickly, place the pan farther away from the heating element. Serve with the warmed barbecue sauce.

## COLA AND GOCHUJANG BARBECUE SAUCE
### MAKES ABOUT 3 CUPS

**½ cup dried fermented Chinese black beans**

**1 liter Coca-Cola**

**½ cup spicy gochujang**

**¼ cup Thai green curry paste (Maesri brand is a good choice)**

**1-inch knob of ginger, minced**

**1½ garlic cloves, coarsely chopped**

**1 cup ketchup**

**2 tablespoons fish sauce**

**1** Soak the beans in water for 1 hour and rinse well.

**2** Add all ingredients to a medium saucepan and bring to a simmer, stirring regularly to prevent scorching.

**3** Reduce the heat to low and very gently simmer the sauce for 30 to 45 minutes, until thick, stirring occasionally. It should taste tangy, spicy and sour. Also, really good. Remove from the heat and let cool. This sauce can be served hot, warm or cold, and keeps in the fridge for 2 weeks in an airtight container.

2 pounds skin-off
pork belly, cut into
6 rectangles

Kosher salt

3 tablespoons
vegetable oil

½ medium onion, sliced

1 medium carrot, cut into
1-inch lengths

½ cup chopped celery

½ cup chopped fresh
fennel stalks

3 tablespoons doenjang

2 branches of fresh
thyme

2-inch knob of ginger,
minced

4 garlic cloves, crushed

2 tablespoons rice
vinegar

3 cups chicken stock

2 cups water

1 fennel bulb, cored and
sliced thinly

1 pound frozen
ddeokbokki, thawed

2 cups washed and
chopped American
mustard greens

¼ cup minced cabbage
kimchi

1 tablespoon unsalted
butter

# Doenjang-Braised Pork Belly with Ddeokbokki

## BY HUGH ACHESON

"It's become more allowable for non-Asian chefs to use more Asian ingredients because the makeup of America has changed," says James Beard award–winning chef and cookbook author Hugh Acheson as we sit down for coffee in his home in Athens, Georgia. "It's not just a lonely ingredient pulled randomly from a culture." Acheson knows a thing or two about these ingredients, particularly those from the Korean pantry. At his restaurant Empire State South in Atlanta, he's added kimchi to both collard greens and rice grits in a natural way.

In this recipe, pork belly is braised to a heavenly state of porkiness with the distinctly Korean union of rice vinegar, ginger, garlic and doenjang, and served with crispy, chewy ddeokbokki. It will make your house smell so, so nice. Acheson's interpretation is not just delicious, but a powerful statement about how Korean flavors can match so well with Southern products. SERVES 6

1 Preheat the oven to 300°F. Season the pork belly all over with kosher salt. Heat a large Dutch oven or braising pot over medium-high heat and add 1 tablespoon of the vegetable oil. When the oil is hot, add the pork belly, fat side down, and sear for 5 minutes, until golden brown. Turn over and sear for another 5 minutes, again until golden brown. Remove the belly pieces from the pot and place on a plate. Spoon out all but a tablespoon or so of the rendered fat and place the pot back on the stove, over medium heat.

2 Add the onion, carrot, celery and fennel stalk, and stir vigorously to scrape up any browned bits on the bottom of the pan. Sauté the vegetables for about 10 minutes, or until softened. Stir in the doenjang, thyme branches, ginger, garlic and vinegar. When the vinegar has evaporated, stir in the chicken stock and water. Place the seared pork belly back in the pot and cover it, but leave the lid slightly askew; bring to a boil. Place the pot in the oven, lid askew, to braise for 2 hours, until very tender.

**3** Bring a medium pot filled with well-salted water to a boil over high heat. Blanch the fennel bulb in it for 1 minute, drain and chill in a bowl of ice water. Drain, pat dry with paper towels and hold.

**4** When the pork belly is very tender, remove it from the braising liquid and set it aside on a plate; loosely cover it with plastic wrap. Skim the excess fat from the top of the braising liquid, then strain it, discarding the solids and placing the liquid back into the pot. Place the pot over medium-high heat. Reduce by one-third. Add the belly pieces back to the pot and keep hot over low heat.

**5** Cut the ddeokbokki into 2-inch lengths and separate them so they are not sticking together. Soak the ddeokbokki in warm water for 5 minutes and then drain and pat very dry with paper towels. Place a large skillet or wok on high heat and add the remaining 2 tablespoons of oil; when the oil lightly smokes, add the ddeokbokki. Let it crisp for about 2 minutes, or until golden brown, then stir and crisp for 2 more minutes. Scoop out the crisped ddeokbokki and add to the pot with the pork belly.

**6** Add the blanched fennel, mustard greens and chopped kimchi, raise the heat to medium and stir well to wilt the greens. Add the butter and stir to gloss. Serve.

# Crispy Tofu Sandwiches with Muchim Pickles and Grape-Jelly Doenjang Dressing

## BY TYLER KORD

Tyler Kord resists convention, down to the broccoli double-decker taco with feta and black beans that put the talented young chef on the New York City culinary map. His No. 7 restaurant is a Brooklyn favorite, and he has a growing empire of No. 7 Sub shops. We've come to love Kord for his bold ideas and smarts with Asian flavors and products. We thought, if this guy could make General Tso's seitan a big hit with the fickle Manhattan lunch crowd, then what could he do with Korean? The answer blew us away when we first tested the recipe: fried tofu with cucumber muchim, and—follow us here—grape-jelly doenjang dressing. Sweet and savory, it's like a Russian dressing on performance-enhancing drugs. (You decide on the kind of performance.) MAKES 4 HUGE SANDWICHES, WITH LEFTOVER PICKLES

**1 MAKE THE MUCHIM:** In a medium mixing bowl, combine all muchim ingredients and let the mixture sit at room temperature for at least 1 hour; leftovers will keep refrigerated for 2 weeks.

**2 MAKE THE SANDWICHES:** Pat the tofu slices very dry with paper towels and season with salt on both sides. Using a deep fryer or Dutch oven, heat 3 inches of oil over low heat. (You want it at 375°F; low heat buys you time so you can continue prepping, but check on the temperature occasionally.)

**3** In a small bowl, whisk together the egg whites and cornstarch until smooth and completely dissolved.

**4** In another bowl, mix together the panko and sesame seeds. In a third small bowl, whisk together the mayo, doenjang and grape jelly.

(recipe continues)

### FOR THE MUCHIM

2 large cucumbers, peeled and sliced into ⅛-inch chips

1 garlic clove, minced

2-inch knob of ginger, minced

1 shallot, finely chopped

2 scallions, sliced thin

½ teaspoon sesame oil

2 tablespoons sugar

½ teaspoon gochugaru

½ cup rice vinegar

1 teaspoon kosher salt

### FOR THE SANDWICHES

1 18-ounce package of firm tofu, drained and cut into 8 slices

Kosher salt

Vegetable oil, for frying

3 egg whites

3 tablespoons cornstarch

2 cups panko bread crumbs

1 cup mixed black and white sesame seeds

¼ cup mayonnaise

½ tablespoon doenjang

½ tablespoon grape jelly

4 Italian hero rolls, toasted

A few sprigs of dill, tarragon and cilantro, leaves picked

½ red onion, sliced thin

**5** Dip a piece of tofu in the egg white mixture and allow the excess "glue" to drip off back into the bowl. Put the piece of tofu in the panko mixture and gently toss until the tofu is completely coated. Put the piece of tofu on a tray and repeat the process with the rest of the tofu. Line another tray with paper towels.

**6** Raise the heat under the oil to medium-high to get it to the target temperature; if you're there already, raise the heat anyway to maintain the temperature as you fry. Fry the tofu in batches that fit comfortably in the fryer until golden brown, about 3 minutes. Remove slices and drain them on paper towels. Repeat with remaining tofu.

**7** Spread a generous amount of the mayo mixture on each side of the rolls.

**8** Put two pieces of fried tofu on each sandwich. Top with some muchim pickles, herbs and red onions and serve.

SO YOU STILL MIGHT BE WONDERING HOW TYLER KORD CAME TO THE CONCLUSION THAT DOENJANG AND GRAPE JELLY GO TOGETHER SO WELL? THE CHEF EXPLAINS.
"Grapes are the universal fruit, so I figured it was a strong guess. If wine goes with everything, then grape jelly goes with anything. And doenjang is probably the closest you could come to making a vegetarian demi-glace, so it just makes sense to add the grape jelly."

# Stuffed Kimchi and Pork Shoulder, Lasagna-Style

## BY EDWARD KIM

At his Chicago restaurant Mott Street (see page 101), chef Edward Kim does this amazing thing where he effortlessly bridges the cuisines of Italy and Korea. A kimchi and slow-roasted pork shoulder dish is one of the restaurant's signatures. Preparing this takes some work and planning, with two 12-hour or overnight steps. But it's mostly unattended, and—as a weekend project, the set piece for a large Sunday supper or dinner party—we think you will love the results. In layering well-seasoned pork shoulder, kimchi and rice, each bite gives you a unique mix of flavors and textures: tender meat; crisped, chewy rice; richness and a sour kick from the kimchi-butter sauce. Kim sells out of the dish every night before the last reservations have even left their homes. SERVES 4 TO 6

1 Preheat the oven to 250°F. Generously season the pork shoulder all over with kosher salt and pepper and place in a large Dutch oven. Cover at least three-fourths of the way up with the stock. On the stovetop, bring the stock to a boil over high heat, cover tightly with foil and then the lid, and place in the oven for 12 hours.

2 Remove the shoulder from the pot—it should be falling off the bone—and let it cool on a large tray. Strain and reserve the stock for another use, or for the next time you make a shoulder. (Stock may be frozen.)

3 Once the meat is cool enough to handle, break it up with your hands, removing bones and shredding up the skin, too, until it's one uniform mixture. Transfer the meat to a large bowl and season it with salt and pepper to taste.

4 In a rice cooker, or on the stove, cook the rice (see page 73). Measure out 5 cups of the cooked rice (reserve the rest, if any, for another use). Transfer the rice to a large bowl and gently fold it to release steam. Season it with the vinegar and then salt to taste. Spread out on a baking sheet and set aside to cool.

(recipe continues)

**1 small bone-in, skin-on pork shoulder (5 to 6 pounds)**

**Kosher salt and freshly ground black pepper**

**1 gallon Pork Stock (page 196) or vegetable stock**

**2½ cups short-grain rice**

**¼ cup rice vinegar**

**6 cups whole-leaf Napa Cabbage Kimchi (page 41)**

**Vegetable oil, as needed**

**3 tablespoons unsalted butter**

**1 cup kimchi juice**

**5** Find a large and deep casserole pan (in the restaurant they use one 10 × 13 × 6 inches); the deeper the better here (this thing has got some serious layers). Spray the pan with a nonstick spray or butter it, line the pan with parchment paper and spray or butter it again.

**6** In the paper-lined pan, lay a layer of kimchi, one leaf at a time, with the leaves slightly overlapping each other. Add half of the shredded pork shoulder. Layer on half of the cooked rice; a few drops of water on your hands or a large spatula will help you smooth out the rice. Repeat with the kimchi leaves, pork and rice. Refrigerate overnight to set the "lasagna." If you can, fill a second pan with some weights and wrap plastic around it. Place it on top of the stuffed kimchi to help compress the layers for easier crisping the next day.

**7** About an hour before serving, preheat the oven to 350°F. Turn the "lasagna" out onto a clean work surface and remove the parchment. Cut the chilled stuffed cabbage into uniform squares. Place a large, heavy skillet over medium-high heat and slick with vegetable oil. When the oil is shimmering-hot, place a few squares of the lasagna in the pan, rice side down. Lower the heat to medium and let the rice crisp up; as it crisps, add 1 to 2 teaspoons of butter to the pan to help color the rice more evenly. When the rice is golden brown, flip the pieces onto a large baking sheet, kimchi side down. Repeat with the rest of the lasagna. Place the baking sheet in the oven to heat through, about 30 minutes.

**8** While the lasagna warms, heat the kimchi juice in a small saucepan over medium-low until it simmers. Whisk in 2 tablespoons of butter to create a sauce. Keep warm, off direct heat.

**9** Serve the lasagna with the kimchi-butter sauce drizzled around the plate.

# Kalbi Meatballs

## BY DANIEL HOLZMAN

The creative process for this recipe went something like this: Daniel Holzman, the gifted chef behind NYC's The Meatball Shop, meets Matt and some chefs and food writers at Penn Station. Budweiser tallboys are purchased. The crew boards the Long Island Rail Road and rides it up to Murray Hill, Queens. Tallboys are drunk. They find a table at Han Joo Chik Naeng Myun & BBQ and order samgyupsal, grilled mackerel and more beers. The banchan is spectacular, and Dan, a longtime fan of Korean cooking, stretching back to his days working alongside a Korean line cook at the upscale Palladin in the '90s, is loving it. The party moves to a charmingly dank little karaoke spot around the corner. Dan sings a Queen (or was it Bowie?) song, and it's basically a mic-drop moment. Dan. Can. Sing.

"I remember Jaelee taking me to a Korean restaurant," he tells us later about his long-ago introduction to the cuisine. "The waitress started putting dish after dish on the table, I started freaking out. I was hooked for life." Though Dan now loves traditional Korean food, he's the meatball guy, so he created a kalbi ball that expresses the distinct flavors of Korean barbecue—soy, sweetness, garlic and sesame oil. SERVES 4 TO 6

1 Preheat the oven to 450°F. In a large mixing bowl, combine the beef, honey, black pepper, sesame oil and vinegar.

2 Combine the pear, garlic, onion, grated ginger, white wine and soy sauce in a food processor or blender and process until smooth. Add the contents of the food processor to the bowl with the meat and seasoning. Add the eggs, bread and bread crumbs and mix thoroughly, but don't overwork. (If it's getting sticky, stop.)

3 Line a large baking tray with parchment paper. Roll the meatball mixture into round, 1½-inch meatballs, making sure to pack the meat firmly. Place the balls on the tray, leaving a little room around each ball.

4 Roast until cooked through and browned, about 20 minutes. Remove from oven and allow to cool for 5 minutes. Serve with scallions and lettuce leaves for wrapping.

2 pounds ground beef (ideally 50/50 short rib and ground chuck)

3 tablespoons honey

1½ teaspoons freshly ground black pepper

2 tablespoons sesame oil

2 tablespoons rice vinegar

½ Asian or Bosc pear, roughly chopped

1 garlic clove, minced

½ white onion, roughly chopped

1 tablespoon grated fresh ginger

¼ cup dry white wine

6 tablespoons soy sauce

2 eggs, beaten

2 slices white bread, minced

⅔ cup plain dried bread crumbs

2 scallions, thinly sliced, for garnish

1 head romaine lettuce, leaves washed and separated for wrapping

**3 cups cornmeal (Brock recommends Geechie Boy brand)**

**1¼ cups rice flour (Carolina Gold recommended)**

**2 tablespoons cornstarch**

**2 teaspoons sugar**

**2 teaspoons baking powder**

**1 teaspoon baking soda**

**2 teaspoons onion powder**

**1 teaspoon garlic powder**

**2 tablespoons kosher salt**

**½ teaspoon monosodium glutamate (MSG)**

**2 teaspoons doenjang**

**3 eggs, beaten**

**½ cup moonshine or vodka**

**2½ cups ice-cold water**

FOR THE PANCAKES

**24 shrimp, halved lengthwise**

**3 scallions, quickly seared in a hot, dry pan until wilted, and cut into 2-inch pieces**

**1½ cups chopped sauerkraut**

**½ cup vegetable oil**

**Jeon Dipping Sauce (page 67), for serving**

# South by South Korea Cornmeal and Shrimp Pajeon

## BY SEAN BROCK

"I'm totally addicted to the flavors of Korea," says Virginia native, multiple James Beard award winner and *The Mind of a Chef* star Sean Brock of Husk and McCrady's in Charleston, South Carolina. Like any professional cook, when Brock visits New York he likes to eat, sometimes multiple meals a night. But first on the agenda is Manhattan's Koreatown: he beelines to Arirang, the tiny second-floor restaurant on 32nd Street, for bowls of his beloved kalguksu, a chicken soup bobbing with dough flakes. (The restaurant has since closed, regretfully.) "For some strange reason the ritual of eating Korean food is very similar to the way I grew up eating in the Appalachian Mountains," he marvels. "Every time I eat at a Korean restaurant, I am reminded of my childhood, because we, too, had huge spreads of food that included lots of pickled, salted and soured condiments." One of his favorites is the crisp Korean pancake haemul pajeon, laced with squid and scallions. In this recipe, Brock gives the classic a Southern twist by adding cornmeal, moonshine and chunks of shrimp, a staple of the Carolina Low Country.

MAKES 4 LARGE PANCAKES; SERVES 8 TO 12

**I MAKE THE BATTER:** Sift dry ingredients (cornmeal through MSG) together into a large bowl. Add the doenjang and rub it in with your hands until a fine meal is formed.

**2** Form a well in the center of the flour-doenjang mixture and add the eggs. Mix with a fork until well combined (lumps will appear, which is OK).

**3** Combine the moonshine and ice water and incorporate it into the batter in thirds, until the batter is wet like crepe batter. Allow the batter to rest, refrigerated, for 1 hour.

**4 MAKE THE PANCAKES:** Preheat the oven to 325°F. In a small bowl, combine 1 cup batter, 3 shrimp, 4 scallion pieces and 3 tablespoons of sauerkraut. Heat a large cast-iron (or oven-safe) skillet over high heat and add 2 tablespoons of oil. Once it begins to smoke, add the batter mixture to form a large pancake and lower heat to medium.

**5** Cook the pancake on one side for 4 to 5 minutes, or until golden brown and crispy. Carefully flip the pancake and place in oven for another 5 to 6 minutes. Check doneness with a cake tester; it should come out clean. Serve immediately with Jeon Dipping Sauce. Continue making pancakes for round two, round three, and so on. Keep the pancakes warm by placing them on a plate and covering it with foil.

# Korean Sloppy Joe

## BY JIYEON LEE AND CODY TAYLOR

Who is the Joe behind the iconic American sandwich the sloppy joe? It's hard to say exactly, but some have pointed to restaurants in Sioux City, Iowa, and South Orange, New Jersey—with typically an unfortunate trademark-law-ignorant cook named Joe being part of the story. While the classic recipe calls for ground beef to be cooked with onions and a sweet homemade barbecue sauce, this Korean version—which comes from Jiyeon Lee and Cody Taylor of Heirloom Market BBQ and Sobban in Atlanta, Georgia (see page 125)—is all about the pork. The simple and delicious marinade consists of some classic Koreatown flavors: garlic, ginger, gochujang, sesame oil and soy sauce. When used in a loose-meat sandwich format, it really can be a surprising curveball to get you out of a weeknight cooking rut. It's best served with a pickle and okra kimchi, which is how they do it in the ATL. **SERVES 2 TO 4**

1  In a large bowl, mix the pork, ginger, garlic, gochujang, sesame oil, sugar, soy sauce and black pepper. Marinate 2 hours, or preferably overnight, in the refrigerator.

2  Heat a large cast-iron skillet over high heat with the vegetable oil. When shimmering-hot, sauté the diced onions for about 4 minutes, stirring constantly, or until soft. Add marinated pork and sauté, stirring, just until fully cooked through, 5 to 7 minutes. Drain any residual fat, if needed.

3  While the pork cooks, toast the buns.

4  Divide the meat and place it onto the buns. Serve, ideally with pickles and a side of Okra Kimchi.

(recipe continues)

**1 pound ground pork**

**1-inch knob of ginger, grated**

**6 garlic cloves, chopped**

**5 tablespoons gochugang**

**1 tablespoon sesame oil**

**1 tablespoon sugar**

**1 tablespoon soy sauce**

**½ teaspoon black pepper**

**1 tablespoon vegetable oil**

**4 hamburger buns**

**1 cup diced onion**

**Pickles, for serving (optional)**

**Okra Kimchi (recipe follows), for serving (optional)**

1 pound okra

8 garlic cloves

1 tablespoon rice vinegar

½ cup sugar

1 cup coarse gochugaru

1 tablespoon onion powder

½ tablespoon black pepper

¼ cup kosher salt

## OKRA KIMCHI
MAKES 1 QUART, INCLUDING BRINE

1  Cut off the stems of the okra and cut the pods lengthwise.

2  Place the garlic and ¼ cup of water in a blender and blend until finely chopped. Add the vinegar, sugar, gochugaru, onion powder, black pepper, salt and 1½ cups of water. Blend until the sugar is completely dissolved.

3  In a large bowl, mix the okra with the sauce. Refrigerate for at least 2 hours. Okra kimchi lasts up to 24 hours in the refrigerator.

# Spicy Late-Night Ramyun Pajeon

## BY CRAIG KOKETSU

This crispy play on kimchi pajeon calls for Shin Ramyun, Korea's favorite instant ramyun, as the base, but any brand of instant ramen will do. A garnish of sriracha, Kewpie mayo and eel sauce—a staple of the sushi bar that is found at Asian grocery stores—adds a decadent final note. When Quality Meats chef-partner Craig Koketsu was testing this recipe, he couldn't keep his cooks away from it. "I knew I had something," he says. He's drawn to Koreatown—his wife is Korean ("My mother-in-law is the best home cook I know!"). **SERVES 2 TO 4**

**1  PREPARE THE PANCAKES:** In a small saucepan, bring 2 cups of water to a boil and cook the ramyun noodles in the water just until softened, about 2 minutes. Drain. Transfer the noodles to a medium mixing bowl. Add the kimchi and scallions and set aside to cool.

**2**  In a separate mixing bowl, whisk the all-purpose flour, rice flour, cornstarch and Shin Ramyun seasoning packet until thoroughly combined.

**3**  In a large mixing bowl, whisk together the cold water, egg, garlic and ginger. Add the dry ingredients and stir gently with a spatula until a thick batter forms. Add the noodle mixture and stir until well coated.

**4**  Heat a large skillet over medium-high heat and add enough oil so that it reaches a depth of ¼ inch. Continue heating the oil until it's hot enough to sizzle a drop of batter instantly. When hot, carefully pour the batter into the pan and, using a spatula, quickly spread the ingredients out to form an even layer. Cook until the bottom is golden-brown, 4 to 5 minutes. Using two offset spatulas, carefully flip the pancake and cook until the bottom is golden-brown, another 4 to 5 minutes. Transfer to a paper-towel-lined plate to drain.

**5  PREPARE THE SPICY MAYONNAISE:** In a large bowl, whisk together the mayo, sriracha, chile oil, garlic, gochugaru and sugar until smooth.

**6**  Cut the pancake into 8 wedges and transfer it to a serving platter, topping with the scallion greens and sesame seeds. Serve with the spicy mayonnaise and eel sauce.

---

FOR THE PANCAKES

1 package Hot & Spicy Shin Ramyun (noodles and spice packet separated)

½ cup thinly sliced Napa Cabbage Kimchi (page 41)

¼ cup thinly sliced scallions

1 cup all-purpose flour

¼ cup rice flour

1 tablespoon cornstarch

2 cups ice-cold water

1 egg, lightly beaten

1 garlic clove, minced

½ teaspoon minced ginger

Vegetable oil, as needed

FOR THE SPICY MAYONNAISE

½ cup Kewpie Mayonnaise

1 tablespoon sriracha

1 teaspoon chile oil

1 garlic clove, grated

½ teaspoon gochugaru

1 teaspoon sugar

FOR SERVING

1 scallion, green parts only, thinly sliced

2 teaspoons sesame seeds

1 tablespoon bottled Japanese unagi (eel) sauce

2 red cabbages
(4 to 5 pounds total)

½ cup kosher salt

½ cup sweet rice flour

¼ cup sugar

3 cups water

3 strips bacon

2 small red onions, thinly
sliced

4 carrots, grated on a
box grater

3 green apples, cored
and thinly sliced

½ cup gochugaru

½ cup fish sauce

3 garlic cloves, grated

2-inch knob of ginger,
grated

# Red Cabbage Bacon Kimchi

## BY EDWARD LEE

Edward Lee is a Louisville restaurateur, fish sauce evangelist, bourbon blender, former *Top Chef* contestant, proud Korean American and author of *Smoke & Pickles*, a cookbook that details his compelling life story. We're big fans of the book *and* the whole Edward Lee Experience. After a career in publishing, Lee worked his way through New York City kitchens and then opened an acclaimed restaurant and beautiful-people scene, Clay, in 1998. After a few hard-partying years, he felt like he'd lost his way. He took a road trip to Kentucky and found himself working as a chef again, combining his Korean heritage with his adopted Southern culture at 610 Magnolia and Milkwood. This recipe is classic Lee, swapping in red cabbage for napa and adding a nice amount of crispy bacon for a really unique texture and salty kick. This recipe makes a lot of kimchi, so feel free to scale down if you don't want it taking over your kitchen . . . and life. MAKES 1 TIGHTLY PACKED GALLON JAR

I  Shred the red cabbage by hand or in a food processor and transfer it to a large stockpot. Sprinkle the salt over the cabbage and toss thoroughly. Let rest for 40 minutes. Rinse, drain well, and return the cabbage to the pot.

2  Make the paste: Whisk together the sweet rice flour, sugar and 3 cups of water in a medium saucepan. Place over medium heat and bring to a simmer, stirring constantly; simmer until the mixture thickens, 1 to 2 minutes. Remove the pan from the heat and let cool to room temperature.

3  In a medium sauté pan over medium heat, cook the bacon until rendered and crisp. Drain the strips on a paper-towel-lined plate, then crumble.

4  Combine the red onions, carrots, green apples, gochugaru, fish sauce, garlic and ginger with the cabbage.

5  Fold the cooled paste into the cabbage mixture. Add the bacon and mix thoroughly. Transfer the kimchi to glass jars or plastic containers with tight-fitting lids. Let stand at room temperature for 24 hours, then cap and refrigerate. The kimchi will be ready in 4 to 5 days, and will keep up to 2 weeks, refrigerated.

# Doenjang and Kimchi-Braised Kale

## BY JIYEON LEE AND CODY TAYLOR

Like Facebook and the Seattle Seahawks, kale has had a pretty huge couple of years. How many "Powered By Kale" and "Beets Don't Kale My Vibe" T-shirts have you seen? Maybe you are wearing one right now. Anyways, we love kale too, and so do our friends Jiyeon Lee and Cody Taylor. This dish, served at Sobban, their Korean American diner in Decatur, takes Southern greens and turns them on their head. The sturdy leaves are cooked down to a tender state with a unique blend of kimchi, kimchi juice, shredded Parmesan, heavy cream and doenjang. It's like Busan meets Bologna, and it's irresistible. **SERVES 4**

**¼ cup vegetable oil**

**1 cup medium-dice onion**

**6 garlic cloves, minced**

**2 cups Napa Cabbage Kimchi (page 41), roughly chopped**

**1 pound kale, washed, stemmed, and roughly chopped**

**1 cup water**

**2 tablespoons doenjang**

**1 cup kimchi juice**

**¾ cup heavy cream**

**1 cup shredded Parmesan**

**1** Heat a large pot or Dutch oven over medium-high heat and add oil. When the oil is lightly smoking, add the onion and garlic and cook, stirring, for about 2 minutes, or until they start to soften and lightly brown in spots. Add the chopped kimchi and cook for 3 minutes, stirring frequently.

**2** Add the kale and cook 1 to 2 minutes, until wilted. Add 1 cup of water, doenjang and kimchi juice. Bring to a boil, then turn down to a simmer. Cook until the kale is very tender and liquid has thickened, about 15 minutes. Add heavy cream and Parmesan to finish. Serve immediately.

# Drinks

## 술

**S**eoul Train: The meticulous lining up of beer glasses filled with lightweight Korean beer and shot glasses of Korean firewater on top, in domino-like fashion. One shot glass is shoved, causing an inevitable chain reaction of crashing glassware and a tidal wave of Korean refreshment to spill over the table—though enough remains in the glass to be passed around and slugged back with a raucous "Geonbae!" Seoul Train: Often where the night out in Koreatown gets a bit fuzzy.

We're sitting in a private room in Dan Sung Sa, a family-run restaurant, bar and karaoke hall in Duluth, Georgia—a tidy Koreatown that is a thirty-minute drive northeast of Atlanta. The rooms are oddly built to resemble an elementary school classroom, with beer-soaked children's crayon drawings lining the walls. Somebody has just sung "Welcome to the Jungle," and a large pan of budae jjigae bubbles nearby while the third (or is it the fourth?) Seoul Train is being lined up.

Some less politically correct–minded have called Koreans the "Irish of Asia" for their inclination to consume large amounts of alcohol with meals—lunches, dinners, snacks, late-night stops at the pocha, one last shot because . . . why not? In Korea, soju is sold at a price cheaper than bottled water, and Matt once counted twenty-two empties and six full on the table at a gopchang restaurant he was visiting in Seoul. In America, where soju is sold for between eight and twelve dollars a bottle, lining a table with dozens of bottles is less common. In Koreatowns around the United States, drinking is still happening, no doubt; it's just not as soju-and-beer centric.

Drinks sections can be kind of throwaways in cookbooks. Not so here; drinking plays too massive a role in the Korean dining experience, so we've included cocktails that will pair nicely with the cooking, and a couple of nonalcoholic options. 끝

1 small seedless watermelon, chilled

2 tablespoons honey, or to taste

Juice of 1 lemon, or to taste

1½ bottles soju, chilled

½ cup Sprite

2 cups ice cubes

# Subak Soju

## 수박소주

### SOJU WATERMELON PUNCH

Talk about a party favor. This simple punch of soju and watermelon juice is incredibly popular in pojangmacha-style restaurants all around the country. At Sik Gaek, a famous late-night spot in Queens, you will see hollowed-out watermelons at almost every table. While the history of the punch's popularity is shrouded in a bit of mystery, it's clear that large amounts of soju poured into watermelons sort of sells itself. We like bringing this over to friend's backyard barbecues. The punch—sweet soju and watermelon brightened with lemon juice—is both refreshing and boozy, and you can always add more soju as the punch dilutes over the course of the afternoon. But we really don't think that is going to happen. SERVES 4 TO 6

**I** Cut off the top of the watermelon and scoop out the guts, placing them into a blender with the honey and lemon juice. Blend until smooth, about 30 seconds to a minute, working in batches if necessary.

**2** Pass the puree through a strainer into a large bowl to remove all pulp, and skim off the foam.

**3** Add the soju and soda to the watermelon puree, stirring to combine. Taste and add more honey to sweeten or lemon juice to brighten, if necessary. Pour the punch into the hollowed-out watermelon bowl. Add ice cubes and allow it to chill for 10 minutes. Set the watermelon in a bowl of crushed ice and serve.

**2 small bottles of Yakult Probiotic Yogurt Drink (2.7 ounces)**

**1 375 ml bottle soju**

**1 can Sprite**

# Yogurt Soju
## 요구르트소주

If you're at the right kind of Korean barbecue restaurant, they'll supply you with Yakult to end your meal: small plastic bottles of yogurt-ish drink, shaken vigorously and then shot down in one sweet, sketchy slurp. Some people like to drink the stuff straight, and Korean parents have been known to pack it in their children's lunch boxes because the good bacteria within has been advertised to aid digestion and cure all sorts of diseases. We honestly think it's best when mixed with things, as in this very simple drink. (It's popular and respectable.) The whole idea is that drinking a bottle of soju is going to get the party started pretty quickly. But nobody wants to drink it straight (unless, of course, there are games involved). Mixing Sprite and Yakult makes it all go down a bit easier. Good for pre-gaming.

Add the Yakult to a large pitcher. (If it is frozen, thaw it out in a bowl of hot water first.) Stir in the soju. Finally, add the can of Sprite, stir to combine well and serve immediately with ice.

# Jameson and Ginger
## 과 인삼 칵테일

For decades, mixing Jameson, a blended Irish whiskey, with a couple blasts of ginger ale from the soda gun has been a dive-bar go-to. But in the past few years, it's gone viral in Koreatown, particularly in Los Angeles. "Koreans are into Jameson and ginger, all day," says Los Angeles bartender Daniel Eun, a lawyer by day and accomplished bar-man by night. While the origin of exactly why Jame-O and ginger is so popular in Koreatowns is unclear, you will find it served as a special in many places around L.A. Eun was on the opening team at New York City's influential bar PDT before moving back to his native Los Angeles. He's currently the general manager of the Normandie Club in Korea-town and is a part of a growing group of second-generation Koreans who are becoming more and more interested in good cocktail bars. Here, Eun offers three versions for all levels of home cocktailing: Basic, Fancy and "Mixology."

### BASIC
Fill a collins glass with ice cubes. Pour 1 to 1½ ounces Jameson into the glass, top with Canada Dry ginger ale and serve with a straw.

### FANCY
Fill a collins glass with ice cubes. Pour 1½ ounces Jameson and ¼ ounce lime juice into the glass and top with good ginger beer (Regatta or Gosling's). Garnish with a lime wedge.

### MIXOLOGY
Fill a cocktail shaker with ice and pour in 2 ounces Jameson, ¾ ounce ginger syrup (see Note) and ½ ounce fresh lime juice. Stir for 30 seconds and strain into a frozen collins glass filled with a hand-cut ice block. Top with soda water and garnish with a slice of candied ginger.

**NOTE:** To make ginger syrup, combine 1 cup sugar, ½ cup ginger juice and ½ cup water and gently simmer for 10 minutes, stirring until every-thing is dissolved. (Ginger juice can be made with any at-home juicer or purchased at your local juice bar.) Strain out any remaining particles from the ginger juice through a fine strainer and cool. Store in the refrigerator.

# CHICAGO
## SLOW CITY MAKGEOLLI

Makgeolli is Korea's oldest alcoholic beverage—a low-proof, milky-white rice wine that was originally consumed by farmers at the end of long days. Good makgeolli is slightly effervescent and dry, with a smooth mouthfeel, and in Korea you can find dozens of makgeolli brands sold in grocery stores, restaurants and taverns. Korean Americans love makgeolli, which is poured from aluminum kettles into small bowls and sipped slowly, paired with particular dishes like scallion and squid pancakes.

---

But much of the good stuff is consumed exclusively in Korea, with just a few brands exported to the United States. Makgeolli contains active yeast and is intended to be drunk fresh—within a week or two of being brewed—and it takes a long time for bottled products to be shipped across the ocean. Facing the reality of spoilage, what's a makgeolli drinker to do? Settle . . . so to speak. The makgeolli that arrives on the docks in the United States has been treated with preservatives (to survive the journey) and the artificial sweetener aspartame (to cover up the taste of the preservatives). It's not bad necessarily, and what most Korean Americans swear by. Heck, many have never tasted freshly made makgeolli. But there is one exception, which is as groundbreaking as it is under the radar: Slow City Makgeolli, a small craft producer based outside Chicago.

You can think of Slow City as the equivalent of the Samuel Adams Brewery, which was founded in 1984 as one of America's first microbreweries. Operating out of an industrial park in Niles, Illinois, Slow City is the only makgeolli brewer located in the Western Hemisphere. Early on, distribution was so limited that the only way to drink the stuff was to visit a Chicagoland H Mart, the independent Joong Boo Market or one of two Whole Foods.

"American people just don't know about this yet, but that is going to change," says retired camera technician John Oh, the president of Slow City, while surrounded by bottles in the company's tiny conference room. Oh started the company in 2013 as a partnership with Baesangmyun Brewery in Korea. Bootstrapping the venture with savings and one full-time employee, he shipped over three large stainless steel tanks and bottling equipment from Korea and started brewing, working in small seven-day cycles. While Oh is clear that his small operation is still in start-up mode—with most of the marketing being in-store tastings at local markets and Korean cultural events—a single sip of his makgeolli reveals just how bright the future may be. The imported stuff is oftentimes flat and slightly bitter, while Slow City is fizzy, light and incredibly refreshing. Chicago chef Beverly Kim serves Slow City by the bottle at her Avondale restaurant, Parachute. And several Korean and non-Korean chefs in New York and Los Angeles have expressed interest.

Oh is optimistic that makgeolli has a future in the United States and is in talks to open a brewery in Los Angeles. The real future of American-made makgeolli may lie in the hands of chefs in search of interesting drinks to pair with their Korean-inspired cooking. We hear that's getting kind of big.

**1 large bottle of soju**

**6 bottles of Korean beer like Hite or OB**

**10 to 12 beer glasses and shot glasses**

# Seoul Train
## 서울 기차 폭탄주
### THE SOJU BOMB ON STEROIDS

You could call this the Korean boilermaker—a shot and a beer tag-teamed with one goal in mind: getting you from point A (clear-headed sobriety) to point B (singing a Foreigner song in front of seventy-five strangers). And as fast as humanly possible. Seoul Train is kind of a drinking game, except that everybody is a winner in the end, and the only loser is the guy who knocks over the glasses early. So follow our instructions and don't be that guy. SERVES . . . WELL, YOU DECIDE

1  On a flat surface that will be OK when deluged with Korea's finest alcoholic beverages, line several beer glasses in a row, leaving a ½ inch space between each glass. Start with 6 to get the hang of it. You can add more glasses as the night progresses.

2  Fill each glass about halfway with beer. Think 2 parts beer, 1 part soju. But it's up to you.

3  Place a shot glass on the lip of each of the beer glasses, making sure they are spaced close enough so that they clink each other (the ones in the photo on the previous spread are spaced too far apart, but don't worry; we moved them closer!). Carefully fill each shot glass with soju.

4  Select a brave participant.

5  Once selected, the brave participant should gently tap the first shot glass, causing a domino effect—with the soju shot landing in the beer with a minimal to typhoon-like splash. Pass the glasses around the table and drink, ideally, in one sip. Geonbae!

# 100-Year Punch

While at PDT, working his way up the ranks to head bartender, Daniel Eun introduced a number of Korean-inspired drinks to the menu. One of those is this punch built around baekseju, or 100-year wine (it's thought that drinking the low-proof beverage guarantees longevity). Widely available at Korean markets under the brand Baek Se Ju, it's a slightly sweet fermented rice wine infused with a number of herbs including ginseng, licorice and ginger. This punch, a definitive party starter, takes some inspiration from the Manhattan—with the sherry-like baekseju adding a really distinct sweetness. SERVES 6 TO 8

Combine the syrup with an equal amount of water. In a large pitcher, combine the bourbon, baekseju, syrup mixture, bitters and tangerine zest and stir. Strain thoroughly into a chilled punch bowl over ice and top with tonic water. Sprinkle with freshly grated nutmeg so that the punch is evenly covered. Allow to chill for 20 minutes and serve.

2.5 ounces of Ssal-Yut rice syrup (or simple syrup)

10 ounces bourbon, preferably Elijah Craig 12 Year Old Kentucky Straight Bourbon Whiskey

10 ounces baekseju

20 dashes of Fee Brothers Old Fashion Aromatic Bitters

Zest of 5 tangerines, finely grated

10 ounces tonic water

1 tablespoon freshly grated nutmeg

½ dried persimmon round, thinly sliced

1 ounce Jujube Tea–Infused Vermouth (recipe follows)

2 ounces Bols Genever

2 dashes Fee Brothers Whiskey Barrel-Aged Bitters

1 cinnamon stick

# Red Devil Cocktail

Jujubes (a type of Korean date) and persimmon are used throughout the Korean kitchen. Here Daniel Eun incorporates both of these sweet and slightly tart fruits in a bold and boozy stirred cocktail. This drink requires you to infuse an entire bottle of vermouth with tea. But don't worry; you can still use this vermouth in a more Eastern-inspired Manhattan or Negroni. **MAKES 1 COCKTAIL**

1   Add the sliced persimmon and tea-infused vermouth to a mixing glass and muddle.

2   Add the genever and bitters, then stir with ice and strain over one large cube into a chilled rocks glass. Garnish with a cinnamon stick.

2½ tablespoons jujube tea (found at Korean grocery stores)

1 375 ml bottle of Vya vermouth

## JUJUBE TEA–INFUSED VERMOUTH

Add the jujube tea to the bottle of vermouth. Close and shake to combine. Set aside for 90 minutes to infuse. Strain out the tea before using.

# Silk Road Cocktail

Don Lee: New York City barman, infusion guru and lecturer on the sensory neuroscience of cocktails. But we know Don best as a proud Korean American who for years has addressed elements of his rich heritage while working behind the stick. Case in point, this wonderfully layered cocktail he created while serving as the opening beverage director at PDT. Aquavit is married with the nuttiness of black sesame, while caramelized simple syrup is an homage to bbopki—a darkened sugar candy that reminds us of burnt marshmallows. **MAKES 1 COCKTAIL**

Stir the infused aquavit, simple syrup and bitters with ice and strain into a chilled coupe. Garnish with orange twist.

**2 ounces Black Sesame–Infused Krogstad Aquavit (recipe below)**

**¼ ounce Caramelized Simple Syrup (recipe below)**

**1 dash Angostura bitters**

**1 dash Peychaud's bitters**

**1 orange twist**

## BLACK SESAME–INFUSED KROGSTAD AQUAVIT

Heat a dry sauté pan on medium-high and toast black sesame seeds and peppercorns, stirring, for 3 to 5 minutes, or until aromatic. Place seeds and peppercorns on a cutting board, in a mortar and pestle or in a spice grinder and pulverize coarsely. Add the warm spices to the bottle of aquavit and shake. Infuse for 10 minutes, then strain through a fine mesh.

**3 tablespoons black sesame seeds**

**10 black peppercorns**

**1 750 ml bottle Krogstad Aquavit**

## CARAMELIZED SIMPLE SYRUP

Add 1 cup superfine sugar and 2 tablespoons of water to a saucepan. Place over medium-high heat and stir until the sugar begins to bubble. Stop stirring and allow the sugar to brown. Once it starts browning, carefully stir in 1¼ cups of water and continue to stir until all the caramelized sugar is dissolved. Allow to cool and bottle.

3 cinnamon sticks

½ cup sugar

¼ cup roughly sliced ginger

6 cups water

4 dried persimmons

Pine nuts, as needed

# Sujeonggwa
## 수정과

### NONALCOHOLIC CINNAMON AND PERSIMMON PUNCH

This sweet dessert punch is a perfect balance of cinnamon, ginger and persimmons, a classic during the fall and winter months. We like to serve this cold and over ice, and always with three pine nuts. Why three pine nuts? It's how Deuki has always served it. It's a superstition. SERVES 4

1  In a small saucepan, bring the cinnamon sticks, sugar, ginger and 6 cups of water to a boil over high heat, then turn down to a gentle simmer. Simmer for 20 minutes, until reduced to 3 to 4 cups. Strain out cinnamon sticks and ginger.

2  Remove the tops of the dried persimmons, rinse the fruit under running water and place them in a large pitcher or glass jar. Pour cinnamon liquid over the persimmons. Allow to steep for 20 minutes, then place in refrigerator. Serve chilled with ice in individual glasses, garnished with 3 pine nuts per person.

# Sikhye
## 식혜
### MALT BARLEY RICE DRINK

2 cups malted barley powder

11½ cups water

1 cup short-grain rice

¾ cup sugar

Pine nuts, for garnish

This cold nonalcoholic barley-and-rice beverage is the way many Koreans like to end a meal. It's very sweet, but the rice and barley add an earthy dimension, and it's really well balanced. We took a group of our non-Korean chef friends to charcoal barbecue mecca Seo Ra Beol in Duluth, Georgia, where we feasted on platters of grilled kalbi and mackerel and doenjang jjigae. When the meal was over, small bowls of clear sikhye were passed around, and everybody was kind of sitting there like, "What are we supposed to do, put our fingers in it?" But once the sweet liquid passed through the groups' lips, it all made so much sense. Ending the meal with a dessert like pie or ice cream is not a popular thing with Koreans, but ending with chilled, refreshing sikhye most certainly is. Note: You will need an electric rice cooker for this recipe. **SERVES 6 TO 8**

**1** Soak the malt powder in 10 cups water at room temperature for about 1 hour, until the powder and water separate, resulting in a clear top liquid. Pour off the clear liquid and reserve it.

**2** Wash the rice in several changes of water until the water runs clear. Soak it in 1½ cups water for 30 minutes, then cook it in a rice cooker.

**3** After the rice is cooked, pour just enough malt liquid into the rice cooker to cover the rice. Reserve the rest of the malt liquid.

**4** Let the rice/malt liquid ferment in the rice cooker for 4 to 5 hours using the Keep Warm function (120°F to 140°F). Do *not* turn the setting to Cook. Look for a few of the cooked rice kernels to float on top, which means that it is fermenting correctly.

**5** Using a fine-mesh strainer, strain the rice mixture in a large bowl and reserve the liquid. Rinse the rice with cold water in a strainer to remove starch. Reserve in a plastic container filled with cold water.

**6** Combine the strained rice liquid with the remaining malt liquid with sugar. This is the sikhye. Refrigerate until chilled.

**7** Serve, garnished with some cooked rice and pine nuts.

# Sweets
# & Desserts

---

# 후식

**A**t Korean restaurants, dessert isn't typically that big of a deal. Small plates of fruit like oranges or Asian pears, chased with a Yakult, usually cut it. With that said, Koreans have an affinity for lingering and loitering after meals, and it's not uncommon to find groups of people, both young and old, standing outside restaurants after a large feast, which sometimes extends to a final stop at a café or a bakery, with sweet breads and lightly brewed coffee as the chosen foods. But even though dessert culture is still evolving (it was only recently that ovens became a staple of the Korean kitchen), we thought it would be a good idea to pull together some closers. This is Koreatown after all, and Americans have an unrelenting sweet tooth. We've got some frozen treats in here, as well as a cookie recipe that might just challenge you a bit. In a good way, of course. 끝

**1½ cups all-purpose flour**

**½ cup rice flour**

**1 tablespoon instant dry yeast**

**1 tablespoon granulated sugar**

**1 teaspoon kosher salt**

**¼ cup milk powder**

**½ cup walnuts or pine nuts**

**½ cup brown sugar**

**¼ cup honey powder or granulated sugar**

**1 tablespoon ground cinnamon**

**¼ cup vegetable oil**

**1 pint vanilla ice cream, for serving**

# Hodduk

## 호떡

### SWEET FRIED PANCAKE

Hodduk is sort of a cross between a donut and a pancake that can be served as a sweet snack or dessert. Though sometimes filled with red beans or sweet potato, our move is nuts, brown sugar and cinnamon, which come together nicely as a gooey center. We typically make a large batch of the dry ingredients (you can easily triple or quadruple this recipe) and keep it in individual containers for easy use. And we suggest serving this with a scoop of vanilla ice cream. **SERVES 4 TO 8**

1  Combine all-purpose flour, rice flour, yeast, granulated sugar, salt and milk powder in a bowl. On the stove or in the microwave, heat ½ cup water until it steams and let it cool until you can place your finger in it; it should be very warm but not hot (about 115°F). Pour over the dry mixture.

2  Knead dough in bowl with your hands for about 2 minutes, or until you form a smooth ball.

3  Cover bowl with plastic wrap and let it sit at room temperature for 20 minutes so the yeast will work its magic and proof the dough.

4  While the dough rises, make the filling. Roughly chop the nuts and mix with brown sugar, honey powder and cinnamon; divide the mixture into 8 piles.

5  Portion out the dough into 8 equal-sized pieces and roll each into a ball with lightly floured hands. Using your hands, flatten each into a pancake. In the center of each pancake, lightly press down a pocket the size of a silver dollar. Add a pile of filling to this center pocket. Close the pancake so the filling is sealed to form a new ball. Gently pat the balls down to form disks (say that three times!).

6  Add the vegetable oil to a large frying pan and heat on medium until shimmering-hot. Working in batches, place a few pancakes seal side down and fry for 2 to 3 minutes on each side, or until puffed, golden brown and cooked through. Place the finished ones on a paper-towel-lined plate to remove any extra oil. Serve with a scoop of vanilla ice cream.

# UNDERSTANDING THE WONDERFUL, SOMETIMES WEIRD, WORLD OF KOREATOWN BAKERIES

With Koreatown crowds lining up for oven-fresh croissants and artfully baked macarons, it's clear that Koreans have fallen hard for the boulangerie and patisserie culture of France. Paris Baguette, which operates over 2,500 locations in Korea and 27 in the United States, is the largest chain, with rival Tous Les Jours a close second. But an afternoon spent ripping into warm dough at one of these joints will reveal that the bakeries are hardly très authentiques.

So, if these French-sounding bakeries aren't French, what makes them Korean? Like many Asian pastries, Korean baked goods downshift with the sweetness and lay off the gas with butter and shortening. Baking in Korea is a relatively new concept, and to this day some Korean houses and apartments are not even equipped with an oven. Not surprisingly, there's been a lot of room for interpretation.

Korean pastries are often sweetened with green tea and honey rather than refined sugar. Croissants can be described as airy rather than flaky. And there's an entire category of baked goods that appear to arrive straight from the kitchen of Dr. Frankenstein. Hot dogs, for example, are often incorporated in the most interesting of ways.

But after many trips to the bakeries of Koreatown, we have fallen hard as well. It just took a little while to figure out what was going on. Here are some of our favorite items to look for:

**MILK BREAD** The packaging advertises the "taste of fresh milk," which is kind of odd because we're talking about bread! But biting into the soft wheat-flour bun reveals a light, creamy flavor. These are also sometimes laced with sweet red beans.

**CROQUE MONSIEUR** A staple of French cafés, this creamy ham-and-cheese sandwich has found itself fully ingrained in the Korean bakery experience. It's typically served at room temperature and wrapped tightly in plastic.

**GOMBO PAN** This streusel bread is also known as pockmark bread because the crumble resembles a less-than-stellar complexion.

**SAUSAGE BREAD AND FRANK PASTRIES** Sweet Italian sausage or hot dogs get jelly-rolled into bread dough and slathered with ketchup and mayonnaise, which is sometimes baked into the dough.

**KOROKKE** This is actually a Japanese word for "cro-quettes" but applied in Korean bakeries to describe deep-fried orbs made mostly from mashed potato, laced with minced meat, vegetables and seafood.

**KOREAN-STYLE SHAVED ICE** Commonly found at Koreatown bakeries, these cups blend ice with sweet red beans (cooked with sugar and vanilla), sweetened condensed milk, strawberries, kiwi or whatever other fruit is in season.

# LOS ANGELES
## SCOOPS ICE CREAM

When Tai Kim creates his ice cream flavors, like cinnamon tahini burnt sugar and maple Oreo, he thinks of it as if he were mixing paint. "Food is like its own art medium," says Kim. He's sitting at a table outside his Koreatown location of Scoops, one of his four Los Angeles ice cream parlors that, for nearly a decade, has grown into one of the city's most-beloved ice cream shops. *Los Angeles* magazine has praised Kim's flavors as worthy of braving the brutal Interstate 405 traffic for, which, if you have driven in L.A., is saying *a lot*.

---

After moving to America from South Korea at seventeen, he attended the California Institute of the Arts to study conceptual painting and live a bohemian life that had him painting by day and, at night, hosting frequent karaoke pop-ups at his live-work studio. Along with cheap beer, Kim served the simple Korean dishes of his youth—kalbi and kimchi made by his mother. Soon, though, the food lit a fire inside of the soft-spoken painter, and he enrolled in the Western Culinary Institute in Portland, Oregon.

It was during a work-study job in the school's supply warehouse that Kim came upon a dusty ice cream maker. With time on his hands (the job called for late-night shifts) he started spinning ice cream using the wide array of ingredients at his disposal—starting with the Baskin-Robbins basics, but moving into more adventurous territory that had the young student playing around with basil–black currant and stinky European cheese. His fellow students loved the flavor tripping, and soon after returning to Los Angeles, he started to look for real estate. "Compton was the cheapest, and this was the second," he says of the first location he opened on North Heliotrope Drive, a scruffy stretch housing a couple bike shops and a large community college. "It was perfect."

Every day Kim writes a menu of around eighteen flavors, new creations and longtime favorites like brown bread, black sesame, and coffee cheesecake. It's a simple, grassroots family business: in a classic Korean-American practice, his retired parents help out at the shop's commissary, while a brother works the overnight shift loading the mixes into the shiny industrial ice cream makers. His niece works the counter many afternoons a week.

The ice cream is made daily, a light and creamy product that's always at a perfect consistency and temperature. Soft and silky. Given his family's heritage and the first shop's proximity to Koreatown, there have been many Korean-inspired flavors sold over the years, including gochugaru sour cream with rice vinegar ("essentially the flavors of kimchi") and the two flavors we've included in the book: makgeolli sorbet and toasted rice.

"Sometimes customers will give an interesting suggestion, and it gives me a challenge," he says of the large suggestion board that hangs in every shop. When asked about the difficulties of fulfilling the requests, Kim pauses with a smile. "I haven't been stumped yet."

2½ cups half-and-half

½ cup heavy whipping cream

⅓ cup sugar

1 tablespoon powdered milk

1 tablespoon toasted rice powder

# Toasted Rice Ice Cream

## BY TAI KIM

While most cooks try to avoid burning anything, Korean cooks embrace the notion when thinking about rice. *Nurungji* is the Korean word that refers to the slightly charred, yellowish rice grains that remain stuck to the bottom of the pot when cooking rice—or, similarly, the bottom of the sizzling dolsot bibimbap bowl. Koreans tend to treasure this super-toasted rice, in some cases soaking it in water and serving as a closing tealike course. Every grain of rice counts.

With this all in mind, Tai Kim—the owner of Scoops in Los Angeles (see page 259)—invented an ice cream flavor that incorporates the elements of burnt rice. He uses toasted rice powder as the focus on the ice cream's strong, though pleasantly addictive, flavor—it's a powerful ingredient throughout Asian cooking, mostly to inject earthy nuttiness into a dish. You can buy toasted rice powder at all Asian grocery stores. This ice cream, which is a Philadelphia style, meaning there is no cooking required to form a custard, is kind of how we want to end all Korean meals. It just works. **MAKES ABOUT 1 QUART**

1 In a large bowl, combine all ingredients until the sugar is dissolved. An immersion blender will really help get the job done.

2 Pour the mixture into an ice cream machine and freeze according to the manufacturer's instructions.

**18 ounces of canned pears in light syrup**

**2¼ cups sugar**

**½ cup makgeolli**

# Pear Makgeolli Sorbet

## BY TAI KIM

Milky-colored and slightly sweet, makgeolli—an alcoholic beverage made with lightly fermented rice—looks like something you would drink for dessert, but it's much more savory than the eye lets on. Tai Kim plays off the drink's mistaken identity with his delightfully refreshing makgeolli and pear sorbet. It's a little different than the fruit-forward sorbets you might be used to; makgeolli still remains the star. But this sorbet is a really great way to close out a Korean dinner party. **MAKES ABOUT 1 QUART**

1 Place pears and their syrup in a blender and puree until smooth. Set aside in a large bowl.

2 In a separate bowl, combine the sugar and makgeolli and stir until the sugar is dissolved. Combine the sugar-makgeolli mixture with the pear puree, then stir in 2 cups of water. Chill in a refrigerator for 2 to 3 hours, until cold.

3 Pour the makgeolli mixture into an ice cream machine and freeze according to the manufacturer's instructions.

# Kimchi White Chocolate Snickerdoodles

## BY ERIC BRUNER-YANG

Erik Bruner-Yang runs the popular noodle bar Toki Underground in Washington, D.C. A few winters ago, Bruner-Yang—who often serves warm cookies to close the meal—found himself with several pounds of white chocolate that had been ordered by accident. Determined to make something of them, the flavor combination that popped into the chef's mind was . . . kimchi.

After several rounds of testing, Bruner-Yang came up with a snicker-doodle that we think is just fantastic: the sweet white chocolate locks into place with the kimchi, with its notes of ginger and underlying hints of fermentation. A dusting of gochugaru offers the right amount of heat. OK. We know this dish is a little dare-worthy, and not really for your fourth grader's bake sale. You might have questioned this recipe from the start. You might still question this recipe. But the blending of flavors (funk, sweet, umami) is pretty much on point. Kimchi actually works in the sweets arena. **MAKES 2 DOZEN COOKIES**

½ pound (2 sticks) butter, softened

1 cup confectioners' sugar

1 egg

2 cups all-purpose flour

½ teaspoon baking soda

1 cup white chocolate chips

¾ cup Napa Cabbage Kimchi (page 41), pureed

3 tablespoons kimchi juice

1 tablespoon finely ground gochugaru

1  In a stand mixer with paddle attachment, beat the butter for 30 seconds, then add the confectioners' sugar gradually. Cream the mixture for 5 minutes until fluffy.

2  Add the egg to the mixture and beat well until fully incorporated. Set aside.

3  In a separate bowl, combine the flour and baking soda with a whisk. Gradually fold the flour into the butter-sugar-egg mixture until just combined. Fold in white chocolate chips, kimchi puree and kimchi juice.

4  Scoop cookie dough into 1 ounce servings (2 tablespoons) and freeze until firm, about 1 hour.

5  Preheat the oven to 375°F.

6  Place the frozen dough balls on ungreased cookie sheets, 4 inches apart, and bake for 11 to 12 minutes, until slightly golden. Remove to a rack to cool. Dust each cookie with finely ground gochugaru.

# ACKNOWLEDGMENTS

This book is dedicated to our parents: Michelle & Sunny Hong and Cheryl & Rick Rodbard. Thank you for teaching us how to eat exceptionally well. But mostly, how to be exceptional people.

The support for this book from the Korean American community, cooking community, food media community and soju-loving community has been overwhelming. There are too many people to thank individually, but here's a shot.

**DEUKI WOULD LIKE TO THANK**
Jesus Christ, my Lord and Savior. None of this matters without You.

My Newsong Church family. I am extremely blessed to have grown up in such a God-fearing and loving community.

Alexander Chang and Peter Yoo. I get scared at the thought of what my life would have been like if I didn't have you guys as my older brothers. Thank you for your wisdom, love and occasional ass-kicking to keep me in check.

Bobby Kwak, Joe Ko, Scott Alling, Jim Yang, Caio Maggi and all of The Circle Group team, from the restaurants to the front office, for your continual support and always allowing me to be me.

My high school principal, Dr. Ed Bertolini, and my home economics teacher, Debbie Gabrielsen. Without Leonia High School, I would not be cooking today.

Michael Bonadies, my former baseball coach turned mentor, who believed in me enough to give me my first start in the kitchen eleven years ago.

To all the chefs I have ever worked for or with. I deeply respect all of you and am honored our paths have crossed.

Finally to Matt. My Jewish-Korean partner in crime. It was a hell of a ride, buddy, and there is no one I would have rather gone on this journey with. Thank you for being an incredible partner, but more important, an even better friend.

**MATT WOULD LIKE TO THANK**
Nadia Cho, you're not simply the best "Korean fixer" on the planet but a dear friend.

To the many family and friends who have been there for me over the years. May we break pajeon soon! Julia, James, Scott, Catherine, Carl, Mari, James, Meena, Adam, Steve Sleeve, Yaron, Ellen and Mya.

Judith Hoetker and Neil Russo, two of the book's biggest supporters and best friends, always up for another round and then a trip to the pocha.

Our lawyer, Jim Rodbard, for reading the fine print and asking the tough questions. You da man.

Our PR pro Robin Insley. Your unwavering support means so much to us.

Our incredibly talented photographer and traveling companion Sam "Ssam" Horine. Thank you for not making this book about the soft-focus bibimbap bowl. You brought our recipes and words to life.

Gabi Porter, thanks for coming through in the clutch. Your good vibes are infectious.

Our illustrator, Michael Hoeweler, thanks for answering our e-mail.

The many volunteer recipe testers. Your honest feedback was incredibly helpful. A special thanks to Mike Traud and the students in the Hospitality Management Program at Drexel University.

Apple Computer and Google Docs. Thank you for being you.

A pack of banchan-loving writers and journalists who helped us find our way: Bill Addison, Zach Brooks, Paula Forbes, Andrew Friedman, Jonathan Gold, JJ Goode, Daniel Gray, Adam Johnson, Matt Kang, John Kessler, Drew Lazor, Joe McPherson, Jessica Sidman, Robert Sietsema and Andrew Zimmern.

Richard Martin, Joe Caterini and all my colleagues at Food Republic and Zero Point Zero Production. Thank you for the support.

Our agent, Angela Miller. Thank you for always being honest with us and running your business with the highest level of integrity and class. You are THE BEST.

All the talented folks at Clarkson Potter, especially Doris Cooper, Danielle Daitch, Erica Gelbard, Carly Gorga, Pam Krauss, Michael Nagin, La Tricia Watford and Aaron Wehner. Thank you for believing in a couple of cookbook rookies.

Our editor, Francis Lam. A beast in this food writing game. Everything you read about this guy is true. Thank you for fully supporting this book—the writing, the photos, the recipes, and most important, Deuki and me. Let that serial comma be placed warmly in your honor.

Chefs! Thank you for the guest recipes, hanging out in Koreatown too late and for thinking about Korean food beyond the kimchi taco. Shouts to Hugh Acheson, Jamie Bissonnette, Danny Bowien, Stuart Brioza, Sean Brock, Erik Bruner-Yang, David Chang, Roy Choi, Amanda Cohen, Vinny Dotolo, Daniel Holzman, Eddie Huang, Edward Kim, Hooni Kim, Tai Kim, Craig Koketsu, Tyler Kord, Edward Lee, Jiyeon Lee, Rob Newton, Pichet Ong, Paul Qui, Eric Ripert, Jon Shook and Cody Taylor.

To my many Korean American friends, old and new, who have taught me about the magic of Korean food and drink. Your continual support and feedback was the only way I could have gotten this thing right: Helen Cho, Mary HK Choi, Daniel Eun, Simon Kim, Jennie Kim, Bobby Kwak, Nari Kye, Debbie Lee, Grace Lee, Sunny Lim, Heather Park, Joyce Park and Dan Suh. And to Jason Ough. It all starts with you.

Deuki. You've been the best partner I could ever ask for on a project. Thank you for always making me feel like part of the family.

And Tamar. Your support, incredible patience and sick copy-editing skills were appreciated every single day, even those when your husband was swearing at the laptop. I love you!

# INDEX

**DEUKI HONG** is chef of the smash-hit Korean barbecue restaurant Kang Ho Dong Baekjeong in Manhattan's Koreatown. He began his cooking career at fifteen as a line cook under Aarón Sánchez at Centrico before heading to the Culinary Institute of America. After graduating near the top of his class, he cooked under David Chang at Momofuku Noodle Bar before spending two years on the line at Jean-Georges. He was recognized as an Eater Young Gun and was named on the Zagat 30 Under 30 list for 2015.

**MATT RODBARD** has written about restaurants, chefs, drinks and music for over a decade. His writing has appeared in *Bon Appétit*, *Men's Journal*, *Travel + Leisure* and on *Tasting Table*, and he currently serves as contributing editor at *Food Republic*. He's the author of *Korean Restaurant Guide: New York City*, a comprehensive guidebook detailing the forty best Korean restaurants in New York City.